A Poetic Odyssey

Scribbulations

A Poetic Odyssey
by Ashley Goodman

Published in the United States
by Scribbulations LLC.

ISBN 978-0-9629311-3-0

*Designed and produced
by Ed Charlton, Scribbulations LLC*

www.scribbulations.com

Cover image:
karenswhimsy.com/public-domain-images

I dedicate this book to my family and friends both living and departed, to my sons, Bruce and David, to my daughter in law Manni and to my grandchildren Avital, Catriel and Malka.

Most especially, I want to dedicate portions of this book to my dear friend Melanie G. Calder who was oftentimes the inspiration and motivating force for what I would consider my best efforts.

Ashley (Ash) Goodman, July 2, 2007

Contents

Lyrics

Foreword

This collection of verse, poems, doggerel and song lyrics is an excursion through my time. It was composed over several decades. The bulk of it during the last decade when I had the time to try to become creative. Most of my life had been given over to making a living and taking care of a family beset by illness. When I gave up trying to be wealthy and nature resolved some of these health issues, I started to compose, poems, lyrics, short stories and plays. I hope you will do me the honor of reading some if not all of my poetry over time. I do not expect you to like all my offerings but then if you find even one poem or lyric to your liking, I will feel fulfilled and gratified. Frankly, I wanted to leave a memorandum of my life and the real me, if such an effort is possible. You will discover that I love life and beauty and women, that I despise liars and hypocrites, and that I have a most peculiar sense of humor; admittedly a strange medley to be contained in a small book. What better way to do this than with a book of verse? Yes, this book was self published. Now, is that sinful? I hope so. I also pray that you will forgive the often idiosyncratic sentence structure, thought patterns and phrasing, as well as the punctuation which I have a tendency to ignore. I believe poetry should be mostly understandable and contain an inner rhythm as well as a provoking thought. Sometimes, I managed both.

Ashley (Ash) Goodman, July 2, 2007

Poems

Odysseus

I, Homer's hero of the Odyssey
Now Reincarnated.
An event long awaited and
Happily, no longer a war hero,
Nor the intrepid sailor of yore.
Meet a simple peasant
Throttled
By life's innuendos:
As fornicator,
Dissembler,
Braggart,
Weary traveler
Whose ass is sore
From pulling his oar.
I shun danger and controversy.
Describe me
As lover of peace,
Hearth and home.
Where I belong.
Loving Penelope
Or the adulating tourist.
I try to be accommodating.
Times are not easy.
You make a drachma where you can.

A Prayer for Myself

I love thee, Ashur,
Child of light.
I forgive thy sins
And deeds not right.
I shall love all creatures
large and small.
Who do not seek
To harm at all.
I shall speak no evil
To anyone.
And rejoice each day
In things well done.
All that is
In harmony with life,
I shall do.
And to myself
I shall then be true.

Virtue

I cannot write happy
verse

No need for me to try to

My only grace is that I'm
terse

Which is a lasting virtue.

Bottom Line

In my supreme arrogance
I forgot
I ascended with Chimps
From Homo Erectus?
An accident of space/time.
Of the quantum paradoxes
Of the subatomic cloud cover
And DNA trinities.
A masterpiece of creation
Obsessed and compulsive

I ask only that you love me.

Making It

Flesh of Sunbeams,
You and I
Falling earthwise from the
sky
Falling earthwise to
Creation
Love and laughter then
Damnation

Praise The Lord

My uncle died yesterday
He was eighty four or five
The funeral was today
They planted him quickly
My uncle had been sick a long time.
There was a certain relief in his passing.

The Rabbi's eulogy was brief, pointed and
Depressing.
He remarked that we were all sentenced to death
Praise the lord, to whom all praise is due.
No comfort for the dead
No consolation for the living
For my uncle a gift long overdue
For my son too soon received.
The following week,
I bought four graves sites
Praise the Lord.

The Blues Singer

There are words never to be spoken
There are memories better laid to rest
There are thoughts to be forever vanquished
If one is to survive the test

Surround yourself with the brightest
Fill your mind with liquid dreams
Bath your soul in the essential fluids
Listen not to the heart as it screams

Happiness is cast with dark shadows
Laughter but for the moment rings
For sadness lurks in the corners
That is what the Blues Singer sings

Heah, lift your head to the sunlight
No point in despairing all this
What else would you have done for the encore
Think what the unborn will miss...!

Immortality Now

Eureka, I have found immortality,
It lives on a plastic disc,
On thin magnetic lines, etched into the disc.
I am recorded,
All of me!
Soon, I will live in a Virtual Reality.
My heart beat and my brain waves will be recorded.
My memories, my fears, my loves inscribed
Even my genomes banked,
To be manipulated.
Reassembled into the perfect me.
Not today. Tomorrow, Yes!
I sing the Body Plastic.

A Tryst

I didn't know I was to tryst
With a water colorist
Painting splashes in the park
Sometimes bright and sometimes dark
But there she was with water colors
Mixing one with several others
Catching autumn leaves on fire
Rainbowed hues to much admire
But then,
I didn't know that I'd be born
Imprisoned in a human form
Moods as evanescent as the light
Sometimes dark and sometimes bright
I didn't know I was to sorrow
With yesterday's regrets; tomorrow!
Where all as promised, Not quite to be.
Embraced by circumstance I could not flee.
It's all a compromise I suppose
Until the day of sweet repose
When, there is no compromise.

The Hubble Constant

DID YOU HEAR THAT?
The Hubble Constant
Is no longer constant.
Constancy does not rule the Universe
We are ruled by Paradoxes
Galaxies are streaming across infinity
At different velocities
Hurtling toward the great attractor
One hundred and ninety million light years away.
To be swallowed up and,
Redigested,
The Ultimate Constant?

Cosmic Truths

Man, the seeker of Cosmic Truths
Delving the celestial outreaches
For the beginnings of gravity.
A seeker of the true faith
Afraid to disavow the ancient myths.
Assured that
"Jingle Bells" is forever,
And "White Christmas" resonated
From the moment of the Big Bing Bang.

That's a heavy gulp.
I stay awake at night
Contemplating reincarnation.
What else is the Senior Citizen supposed to do?

The Brain

This mass between my ears,
Organized for self destruction
I am driven to extremities
But forever held to the center
One stupidity follows another
I reinvent myself,
Repeatedly,
In the same patterns
This assuages my fears
This dampens my grief
This nurtures my regrets
I seek the same images
I replay the same scenarios
The characters are not different
The shadows are the same.
The consequences vary slightly
I am bound to the wheel.

Unbounded Bliss

Unbounded by time and space,
No margins of definition
I soar into that limitless grace
Of Bliss, a realm of atoms,
Of spinning electrons
Of memories and imagination
Of my infinite union
With the universe
A connectivity without locale,
Holographically recorded
In massless photons
An interference pattern
Imaging the un beginning
And the un ending
From which I have evolved
To which I am evolving.
I am constantly renewed,
Refreshed on the other plane
Where I am eternal.
I share this eternality
Here and Now
With all who seek Bliss.

Renewed

Immured twixt sand and sky
Cottaged by the sea we lie
Nerve endings to cure
In the sun's rays
In the salt sprays
Strident nagging sounds be done
We want wave whispers, a gull's cry.
With our omniscient sun
Renewing, oh to be renewed
We strive
Is it not enough to be alive?

Youth

The Sun illumines
what the eye doth see.
Without the sun,
we would not be

But the Sun is fragment
of that light
That sheds the darkness
from the night

And gives us pause
to see the day
And celestial mysteries
far away

And he who seeks
eternal truth
Is but a seeker
of undying youth

For in the enigma
of the sky
The planes of immortality
doth lie

Where we are destined to
ascend
Our energies with the oversoul
to blend.

Re Creation

Space time... world line,
spinning endlessly into the red shift

Go we voyagers into the infinity of curved space,
back to the beginning.

No maps to chart our journey, dead reckoning to
an ice age.

A word,
a night,
a day,
the spins of time,

Harken,
the eternal silence.

Immortality Revisited

Shivering,
I came upon the mountain top above,
Shivering,
I will go into the valley below.

A day will pass,
And who will remember,
That I walked the mountain top,
And descended into the valley.

It does not matter who.
I have learned that I am immortal.
That I die and I am reborn.

Over the centuries I have come and gone,
And come again.
I have lived many lifetimes.
Sometimes, as the fool,
Sometimes as the wise man,

When I am gone from here,
I reenergize on some celestial plane,
Awaiting rebirth, to requite for my sins,
To become a better born.

I give no living memories to these events.
Perhaps, that is my problem.

Resurrection

Closet cleaning,
I found a packet
Of old photographs
A jumble of
Forgotten Faces
Ancestral reflections
Of stolen light
Reminders of
The by gones.
I wondered,
Studying their faces,
Will we, one day
Clone a photon
Of these images,
Return them
To the moment
Of their creation
And ask,
“What do we do
With you?”

Just another horror
to contemplate.

The 5th Dimension

In how many dimensions do I reside?
Ingesting unseen energies and
Charged by a billion chemistries.
An organic battery of raw emotion
Both male and female congealed
In a triuned brain.

Damn Biology and its gene pool
Damn physics and its quarky shadows.
I cannot define myself there.
I want that old time religion
I am wolfman, son of the beaver,
My cousin is the coyote.
My brother, the bear.

My gods dwell in the trees and rocks
Everywhere!
Each day, I bless or curse the Sun
As it feeds or saps my strength.
I am earth bound, yet my spirit soars
I am not contained in a Book...
Like the atom, I am free to wander
In all dimensions,
And worship as I please.

Mother's Side

If you are hungry
Let me feed you.
If you are lonely
Let me fill your nights.
If you need hope
Let me lift up your eyes.

Here stand I, Mother Earth
Breasts in hand, legs akimbo
An offering.

Lie upon my bosom,
Dwell between my thighs
Like the multitudes before you.
Am I not forever?

Let my womb be your sanctuary,
My fruits your nourishment.

I was born to serve you.
Listen, my heart throbs in your presence

Yet you ravage me,
You tear at my sinews,
Gnaw upon my bones
I am desecrated by your works.

My seas are pools of excrement
My forests ripped from their roots
My air and waters polluted with your greed

Yet, I was triumphant in my creation!

I was imploded in the no time,
Out of a dust cloud,
A boiling rock unfurled from
Star Waste.

Like you, I am without recall
I am neither what I was
Nor will be as I am.

Listen,
There have been billions before you
Endless species in the laval tides,
Mindless numbers consumed
in the sun's furnace,
Frozen in the cloud cover,
rinsed in the acid rains,
Digested in another's chemistry
Until you became as you are.
A permutation on life's tape,
A creature of improbability

I did not offer eternity,
just a moment in time and space.
A beginning and an end.

Though, I have birthed you and
Nursed you and
Cursed you with a brain
You have sought revenge upon me,

You think me without feeling,
without intelligence
A watery rock afloat
in the endless firmament
Do you imagine, I cannot defend myself,
Lay waste my ravagers?

Look to my tortured history,
It is buried in my rocks,
In my desert sands, in my tar pits.

I have dissolved atmospheres,
and made floods.
I have spewed cloud covers
and disdained my lover,
Ashur, the Sun God.

All manner of plagues, I have sent
Until the extinction was complete

Do you celebrate my presence?
Sing paeans to my bounty?
Worship at my altar
as did your ancestors before you?
Not at all.
You contrive strange gods
lost in the firmament

You forget, this is your home.
Your only home,
The home of our children.

Guard it well, or it will Perish.
But I promise nothing.

Tour Guide in Arizona

Two hundred million years
Rolled off your tongue,
As if they were yesterday
Not three million times
My life span
What if I said to you,
A part of me, molecule or two
Once swam in those nameless seas
That ebbed and flowed upon these arid lands,
Would you have laughed?
When I stand quietly,
Contemplating those sedimentary rocks
Layer upon layer stratified
Into fossilized memories of vast extinctions.
I despair, of finding a record in my genomes,
Of these events.
Yet we were there,
Waiting to be born
And to be extinguished.

Waiting for God to stir the pot,
To add the salts and tinctures
That give rise to life and assuredly to death.
The irony is, that I came upon this
Prospecting good times
In the arid zone.

Confession

"Do you know what I love best?"
A strange question
I thought,
She's chiding me.

Surely,
She would say her children,

I wanted to say,
"Your Children".

But, I hesitated,
Unwilling to preempt the answer.

Once,
She had confided in me
And expressed regrets.

Now,
I wanted her to tell me
What she loved best.

I said,
"No mama, what do you love best?"

"I love nature best,
The flowers, birds and trees,
I love best" she said.

I understood her,
For the first time.

I felt privileged,
Taking her confession,

Saddened too,
That I had not understood this
Before.

It explained so much.

It is time
Now,
For me to ask myself
The same question,
Before the before.

Yet, for me,
The answer is not that clear.

Wrinkle Proof

Take it off this wrinkled skin
I don't wish to be seen in
This shawl of washed out grayish hues
A garment that I did not choose
I want the shinning garb of youth
Not something old and so uncouth
I'm ashamed to wear it.

It strikes me that its quite unfair
That from my body, I dare not tear
This outer garment I deem unfit
For to my mind it does not fit
The image of myself, I see
As tall and youthful as one should be.
I'm ashamed to wear it.

So to the cosmeticians I shall wend
For those treatments with the blend
Of soft massages and exotic oils
To repair what nature soon despoils.
Must I accept with proud grace
This grim heritage of the human race.
I'm ashamed to wear it.

Why can't science now invent
The kind of skin that's heaven sent
The skin that cannot dry or peel
And retains it texture, like stainless steel?
I am certain that from a tree
One can make a skin that's wrinkle free
I'd be thrilled to wear it.

The Dance

She sat, nodding quietly
As if riveted to the chair;
An old hen
Waiting for an egg to drop
Resisting the spell of the beat.
Not a tremor, not a twitch
Let's dance, I suggested.
She declined, demurely
Lowering her eyes, softly
She had surrendered to the years,
I resented that
I resented her serenity
I resented her acceptance
I wanted to scream
Dance you witch,
Dance until you die.
Dance until your eyes sting
And the rivulets of sweat
Saturate your armpits
And burn your pores
Dance until your mind and feet become one
Dance until there is only the dance
The ecstasy and frenzy of the dance
Don't you understand!
The man has grabbed your ankles
He will pull you under
Fight him!
Fight for your ankles!
Fight for your ankles!
Instead, I said nothing, and
Shook the thoughts from my head.

The Flight

There is a quietness on the meadow
There is a stillness on the land
As I stand upon the hillside
Watching nature's work at hand
As I stand upon the hillside
Drinking in sweet air
I let my mind go wander and sail without a care
Across the meadow's lushness
Perfumed with living things
My soul cannot contain itself and
Joyfully takes wings
To soar mid cloud filled skies
To dance before the trees
So filled am I with wonderment and
Wild ecstasies.

Manhood

He sat in his office chair
Head hunched into his shoulders,
A voice barely audible
His right hand shook uncontrollably
"I still can hit a golf ball", he boasted.
I smiled and uttered some banality
"How long have you been sick?"
I mumbled
Rebuking myself immediately
For open ending the conversation.
He wanted to talk,
To speak of himself, of his past.
There was no future,
A dark tunnel, very dark.
I sat there quietly,
Drenched in his and my own remorse.
Listening, Listening.
Later,
He shuffled to the door to show me out.

The Urge

There is within me this urge;

To greet each day with a shout of joy
And grasp the Sun to my bosom and plant
A kiss on its fiery brow

To tumble in the fluff of cloud stuff
And like a ball of cotton candy
To become devoured by ten thousand loving Women

To zoom beyond the stars
And lose myself in the galaxies of other worlds
And other promisings

To run wild between raindrops
Never to get wet
To play cowboys and Indians until
Skies darken and Supper waits

There is within me this urge
To learn about everything
And to teach this to the world

To love and savor the varieties of life
To the center of my being,
So that when
I am gone ten thousand years
Someone may say
He lived not in vain.

Myth

Myth has it, that,
From a compacted sphere of space and time,
Our cosmos came on line
A blow, that was heaven sent?
And space and time were rent
While gaseous clouds collapsed
Elements composed, and were dispensed

8 billion years may have passed
When stars were formed
And then collapsed
When suddenly, as if by design
From out of slime and strife
Emerged the matter we call life

The Truth Incarnate

Forgive me,
I was not listening to you.
I don't know why,
I don't listen to you.
It must be some defect in me
Not to listen.
Perhaps, I hear or sense some criticism
In what you say
Or in the way that you say it.
It may be that
I do not want to confront the truth;
It is too unruly, the truth,
Not subject to logical thought
Or analysis.
It distorts reality
The truth does.
It makes you question your belief systems,
The grout that holds your life together...
Called to question.
No one has the right to do that!
Not even God.

The Children of Chernobyl

I looked for the children
They were not there
I looked for the children
I did not despair

I was told they were hiding
In the forest abiding
Awaiting the bell for all clear

But the bell never sounded
The bell never pealed
Until after the rains
When all was revealed

When the bell clamored loudly
To summon the few
Who witnessed the horror
And quickly withdrew

The leaves had all seared
And crumbled to dust
The children had all withered
And were convulsed into must

Nothing remained
But the blood and the gore
Nothing remained
But the deadly down pour

The rem and the rad
Were not finished as yet
They were swept to the heavens
And carried by jet

Across the wide heavens
Sped the rem and the rad
To the chatter of geigers
It was all very bad

The air became poisoned
Not fit to be breathed
The water became poisoned
Not fit to be drunk
The food became poisoned
Not fit to be eaten
And dead was the land for ten thousand years
.

A Killing Reminder from Serbia

There is something in me,
That hates you
And everyone like you.
It is not logical,
But I do not examine it,
This hatred
Because, perversely,
Hatred makes me feel superior
And righteous.
My blood is pure and sacred
My Gods divine
It becomes necessary for me to hate,
And kill, something, someone,
Whose mere presence
Defiles my purity and
Mocks my Gods
"Kill, in order to live"
A survival mantra
When we hid in caves,
Coveting our women and our fears.
It is genetic now, this hatred,
You are the perpetual stranger,
Your face offends me,
Your voice, an anathema
Your presence a threat.
We must settle old scores,
In this battle for life,
It is you or me, then and now
Time has altered nothing.
Hatred lifts the axe a little higher,

Propels the stone a little faster,
The blood exults in the kill.
I do not see that in killing you,
I am killing myself,
And the generations that follow.
It does not matter; the arguments.
Killing is something I enjoy,
And practice. Praise the Lord.

Lost Encounter

I live from day to day
Said the girl with the hazel eyes
Ablaze with glory of herself
Her hair red and abundant
Then we can never be, said he
Catching glimpses of his regret
In the picture's glass behind her

How so? She flashed
Because I am yesterday
And with you there are no tomorrows.

The Promise

And so she was lost to him,

She said because he failed to keep his promise

He said he had no recollection of this promise

And she could not remember it either except

As some half recalled memory

Yet she swears it is true, because

Otherwise, why would she remember it.

He has no answer for this except to say

I have lost her,

As I have lost so many things before.

But it is she whom I valued most.

Now she is gone and the promise remains.

Goodbye

Sorry, we were not there to say Goodbye.

We all fear that big step across the line

Was it yesterday we met in younger times?

The blood would boil hotter then
and watching you flick
wrist shots across the net
was pure pleasure.

From what better place to foot fault,
where you were king.

Yes, you were a strong presence,
with wit and insight not easily challenged.

Always to be recalled,

Bon Voyage! Dear friend.

Fear

It is easy for you old man,
To lose your ego and desire
Among the stars.

Contemplating the great illusion
That seems a thousand
But is only one.

For me, in the arrogance of my youth,
I am propelled by hungers
You can only vaguely recall.

I need the love of women,
The envy of men.
I must be celebrated
So that my success shines a beacon
For the world to behold.

I cannot sit, crossed legged,
Awaiting for the epiphany.
I cannot sit awaiting the beacon.
I cannot shed my ego.

The Cat

Listen, the cat's crying!
Not remorse, Hunger!
She wants to come in
Her predations done,
I'll open the door.
She comes home to rest
From the terror she spreads,
From the death she inflicts.
How human!
I wonder, is heaven any better?

Cope Night

Stop it,
I don't want to listen
While you recount your sorrow,
I've enough of my own
Without yours to borrow
Go peddle your grief
Somewhere else,
Or park it on a shelf
And let the bugs eat it.

No, I'm not without sympathy.
Should I be?
Listening to these endless details,
As if You were the only one
Plagued with such travails.

I'm sure,
That in this wide wide world
There are those who are more accurst.
Than You or I,
And deservedly.

Song of the Seas

Sing me a song of the seas, old son
Sing me song of the seas
Let the words ring wild and free,
Like the wind and waves of the seas

Tell me tales of the sailing men, old son
Of the men who sailed the seas
Of the rotten life and the bitter strife
Of the men who plied the seas

Oh grand adventure there was, old son
Athwart the blustery seas
For the men who brave the vagrant wave
Sailing the roving seas.

Then spin me a yarn of widow and wives, old son
Of the wives and widows of the heartless seas,
Who lived and cried by the frothing tide,
When their husbands offed to the seas.

Now when you tell the tales, old son
Tell the tale of the orphaning seas
Of the day I fell into the watery hell
As my ship sped acrost the seas?

Nary a tear was shed, old son
For the man who fell to the seas
Neither the crew nor the Cap, cared not a rap
For your father who drowned in the seas.

Too Young

She died in the Spring
The sweet young Thing
The grass didn't grow
The trees bent low
Their grief to show

She died that year
The sweet young dear
The birds took wing
And forgot to sing
Tho it was spring

She died that day
The sweet young fey
The skies turned gray
As they laid her away
On that sad, sad day

Now the eyes that smiled
Will smile no more
The voice that warmed
Will warm no more
The world's not the same
It is filled with pain
When she went away...

On that April day.

The Last Snow Storm

At my age, I sometimes wonder,
Whether the last snowstorm will be my last
Snowstorm.
I suspect we are allotted so many snowstorms,
So many raindrops, so many hot sticky days and
Nights, etc. and that's it.
We use up our portion and buy the farm.
The prospect doesn't frighten me, exactly.
I have often come to the edge
To simply challenge the fates,
Even the possibility of failure has an allure.
I wanted an adventure a day.
To enrich my life, the consequences
Were secondary to the event.
Yes!
A big snowstorm or tornado would do,
In a pinch.
That is why I took to writing poetry.
Death stalks the arrogant writer of verse.

Hermaphrodite

What the hell do you mean when you say
"I am a hermaphrodite?"
Is that one of those new fangled religions or
somethin?
If it is, I do not want to hear nothing about it
So lets get the definition straight.
Shoot!
I'm sure it will give me indigestion over my
indigestion
And I'm taking enough Malox
To gas-kick my butt over the moon
Whatayahmean, it means you got both sex
organs.
Where?
Yeah, that is a question.
Don't mess with me brother or sister.
You are looking at a big fist here
Hey man, I heard about fish with fur
And I didn't believe it either.
Cause,
I got to see one to believe one
I'm one of those skeptical types
What?
You mean you are going to show me.
The damn thing, things.
Well, I'll be damned.
Yup!
I guess you are right.
I've never looked real close at those parts
Before.

I’m a private person, well private parts
Means exactly that to my thinking.
But, it looks like the real thing, things,
Kinda!
Does that mean you can “f” yourself
And give yourself a baby or something?
No, it doesn’t mean that.
To bad,
Now that would be real strange.

A Mother's Notion

My mother's notion of a good meal
Had nothing to do with gourmet principles.
For her it was a matter of time.
She was a working woman and so time
Bore heavily on her mind
And she tried to use it wisely,
She would often ask, enthusiastically,
My opinion of her cooking.
As a dutiful son who loved his mother,
I would reply, enthusiastically,
"Delicious mom, de--licious."
My mother would beam.
I liked to make her happy
"Guess how long it took me to prepare it?
She would insist?
Dutifully, I would reply, " Gosh mom, I have no idea",
Although, I knew the answer by heart.
"Two, minutes", she enthused.
" Two minutes, incredible", I would intone,
With a murmur of incredulity in my voice,
As I surgically excised burnt portions from my fare.
Yeah, I miss her cooking.

Booth in the Corner

There is a booth in a corner
Hidden away
It sells dreams of travel to lands
Far away
I have tried to find it time and a-gain
Yes,
I have tried to find it but
It was all just in vain
I wanted to escape to a joyous land
Where there is sunshine and beaches
Filled with soft sand.
Yes, I wish to escape to more pleasant clime
While I am young of heart and
There still is some time.
Where is this booth in a corner?
Please let me know
Because, I'll buy you a ticket
So you too can go.

Don't Be Unreasonable or The Captive

Don't be unreasonable, I ain't goin anywhere
It's here, right next to you that I intend to stay
Maybe you've got some other plans,
that I don't know about
Well, let those plans just slip away
And don't have another doubt
I've fought too long to make you mine and keep you
Here at home.
There is one thing that is certain, dearest one,
You have no room to roam.
No, I don't, think of you as a piece of fluff
I know what I have got.
Yeah! Sweetness, you are my precious honey pot.

If you think you've got another beau, well,
get rid of the ugly bum
Otherwise he's goin to find he's on his way to hell's own
Kingdom-come.
Oh, I suppose you like to think that
you don't belong to me,
But honey pot, I'm telling you, I won't ever set you free.

Now, get it clear, I said I won't and that's because
you're mine,
Yesterday, tomorrow, now and until the end of time.

No, I'm not being unreasonable that conclusion is the damnest lie
And, I'll remind you once again I'm not some simple toy
So don't think to fool with me, don't, don't even try.
You're looking at one tough old bird and not some country boy
Just remember one damn thing that you belong to me
And not to that other guy.
Now, come on over here, I'm goin to teach you how to snuggle
Yeah, go ahead, I love it when you squirm and when you try to struggle.

Peace

Have you ever thought what peace would bring
If man made love not war
I'm sure it would make the angels sing
And maybe even more.
We got to give love a chance there is no other way
It's the only alternative we've got
If it's life, not death that must hold sway.
It's a crime to let your kids grow up
Then send them off to war
Where the death machines chews
Them up
And the Devil keeps the score.
All men and women throughout the world are genetic
Twins
No matter where or to whom they're
Born
And in a senseless bloody war,
No one ever really wins.
And everyone is compelled to mourn.
You can preach an end to a senseless
War.
But, If the President and his inner circle
Really want to have it.
It's another useless chore.
For they will create the reasons for it.
And the patriotic minions, without a moment's
Hesitation.
Proudly, send their children off to death or
mutilation.
As they lust to kill each other
Maybe that is why the angels
Sing, a dirge at one another.

The Jain (A Chance Encounter)

Inspired by a conversation with a Dr. Sha

He did not mince words
Speaking in a low slow consoling voice
Allowing his words to melt along the edges
Before they pierced her heart
"You have breast cancer", he said
"You need therapy immediately."
The echo of his words pounded
In her head and went rebounding
Down the generations of her
Matriarchal line,
Hammering at every synapse.
She shuddered and started to sob.
In a comforting voice, he added
"It is a curable cancer.
Not to despair."
Her mother had died of breast cancer.
She mumbled, "It's genetic.
There is no hope"
He said something about modern medicine
Having come a long way and finding serenity was
Essential if she was to survive the treatment.
She did not care-for his feeble reassurances,
But his words had struck a bitter core,
Igniting an anger that had been gestating
for a long time.
She replied, "Finding serenity", hah!
Not in our world.
This world moves so fast today, serenity in this
Spiraling clutter on noise and violence
is out of the question.

She continued, (he noted that her
Bitterness had deep roots, very deep)
Serenity is a mere blur on
The horizon, not accessible.
Visible, perhaps, but only as an ink spot,
“Serenity is not its only victim,” she continued.
“Everything seems to caught up in this
Marijuana madness.”
She was energized by her subject.
“Listen to at our contemporary music”, with its
Raucous voice and inherent violence
And the brutality
In our movies.
He nodded in agreement.
Do you realize that, compromise, forgiveness
And kindness, all have all been killed off
With a single phrase, “Make my day?”
“Dig some rap, (emphasizing dig) and
Be buried under an avalanche of ugly language.”
As she spoke she had this vision of molecules and
Cells exploding,
Bursting everywhere,
“Hell, where do I belong in this frenzy?”
She sobbed again, her voice breaking.
“But you see,” the doctor continued unruffled,
“I am a Jain.”
She looked at him, startled
By this strange confidence.
She knew what a Jain was.
Not some anonymous nobody
With a name tag tied to her toe.
He was a member of an ancient

Indian religion that insists that
All life forms are sacred,
She had read somewhere that
A pious Jain will have the sidewalk swept clean
Before them for fear of killing
Any life-form.
And here she was before him,
But her resentment was
Transparent.
This living specimen of Jain,
It had
Come to speak of her of death.
She hated the messenger.
Yes, he looked and sounded human,
He was without horns and appeared vulnerable.
Sensing her scorn, he rose solemnly from his chair
And spoke proudly,
"To seek serenity is an essential part of our faith."
He paused, allowing the words to resonate.
At that moment she felt chastened.
"Do you have a God?" she murmured.
"No, there is no God in my religion," he said
"We have only holy men and the last one
Died 2500 years go."
"How do you find serenity then?" she asked,
Querulously.
He responded quietly and with dignity.
"There are people and places that give you
Serenity.
You must seek them out for
They are Holy."

Not Enough Time

There was never enough time for you and me
It was OK at first
Then it got complicated
The children came so fast
Both of us felt harassed
Not a good way to enjoy a family.

Life's problems settled hard on us
And I took to drink
What money I did make
The bartender took
And,
I was too ashamed to admit
That I had shirked my family
Responsibilities.

I cried like a baby when you threw me out.
I knew I deserved it
You were the bread winner
And,
I was the drunken sot.

Well, honey that's all changed
I found God and he has made a new man
Of me.
I want to come back and prove my worth.
I've got a good job and saved some dough
If we pool our incomes and go slow
We can rebuild our lives together and have a proud
family
To show the world we made it.

What do you mean you don't believe me.
You can smell alcohol on my breath?
You lie, vodka doesn't smell.

On Reflection

Exhuming the past in my mirror
And mixing it with the present
I view the fossilized remains of self.
I seek a callow youth,
I am he standing on the street corner
Of the old neighborhood
Listening with rapt attention
To the tall tales of exotic escapades,
In the whorehouses of Scranton, Pa.
Drenched in wonder,
I shiver involuntarily.
I have not come far from those days
Though long in beard and tooth
I see through dimmed eyes
Those bones of self, bleached in the sun's rays
The errant flesh is gone, before its time,
Misspent in the whorehouses of the mind
Too much testosterone in those memoried cocktails
For any man to manage.
But where has this madness gone?
Why!
To the center of the earth
To be boiled in the magma of desire
Always, hidden beneath the crust.

Scar Tissue

What is life anyway?
Getting and spending.
Rearing children
Protecting them,
Educating them
Watching them destroy
Themselves
With some indiscretion.
A bad marriage,
A dumb career choice,
A sniff of the wrong stuff.
Some damn disease that wasted them.
Maybe you are one of the luckies.
A good marriage,
Wonderful children
A fine job
No serious afflictions.
Look,
Great poetry is composed of scar tissue
Scar tissue scraped from the souls
Of its victims.
Scar tissue is the rest and residue
You leave to the world, when the bowl empties
After vomiting the pig's sphincter.
If nothing else,
It surfaces from the grief you
Survived.

The demolition of loved ones;
The degradations you ignored;
The despair you conquered.
The forgiveness that mellowed you;
This is the source of great poetry
Great poetry is etched in the keloids on your soul.
You dig it out with your teeth.

If You are My Poem

You ask that I write you a poem.
Why should I?
For as Walt Whitman said,
“You are my poem”.
If I need one, I shall
Appropriate you.
I shall pin you
To my bedroom wall
Or better yet,
To my refrigerator door.
I shall hold you there
With a powerful magnet.
There you shall remain,
An imposing figure,
Draped on my refrigerator door,
Covering memories of childish pictographs.
When someone asks,
“Who the hell is that
Hanging from your refrigerator door?”
I shall reply, “that is my poem”.
Some will be pleased
That I have shown such imagination,
Sealing a living being on my refrigerator door,
As a poem
Others will be horrified,
By the brutality of the deed.
But that is life,
You cannot please everyone, nor should you try.

I shall assure them
That when you are hungry
You need only open the door
For food and drink.
Some spoilsport will observe,
"But that is not possible".
I shall scoff and say to him,
"All things are possible if you are my poem."

Look But Don't See, Ok?

I got to turn off now.
Close down the observatory
Stick my head in the sand
Or up my ass.
I've nothing to write about.
I've turned off.
I refuse to look,
I don't want to see
What the hell is there to see?
Shit's burning
All over the world.
Death and destruction
All over the world.
Hey, the terrorists are coming.
The terrorists are here.
They are in Washington, DC
There is no exit.
They control the exits
But I want out.
I won't look.
I won't smell the moral decay.
I wont pretend it will come out OK.
OK?
I don't want your approval.
I can't hear your applause.
Go away, get lost.
Am I supposed to cry for the dead,
The mutilated, the earthquake survivors,
The victims of the tornadoes,
The sick, the needy, the widows.

The orphans,
The war crime victims?
What the hell for?
I'll cry for the Bushies, the Saudis,
For Saddam.
I'll pray for them; forgive them
Their trespasses
And get on with my life.
My advice to you is to pray.
But to whom you ask?
How to hell should I know?
I can't find the right one.
There are multiple choices.
So take your choice.
Don't you see?
They or it are all the same
Would he, she or it have it any other way?
Trouble, grief, sin, despair wont go
Away.
Not for God's sake.
Don't you see
It is supposed to bring us closer.
Because,
There will be more tomorrow,
The same shit.
And the day after tomorrow,
Ad infinitum.
It identifies us.
It isn't OK, or not OK you know,
It just is.
The word OK isn't in life's dictionary.
The words death, destruction,

Mutilation, despair, and hopelessness are.
They are there in every sentence, in every speech.
Listen,
The terrorist are coming.
Fear, they sell fear.
In every other word, and
Even the most powerful succumb.
To fear.
It distorts reality or makes it's own
We titter in our bomb shelters,
We shiver in our wooden shacks.
We revel in our paranoia.
How about love, you ask?
How about faith, hope and charity?
And sanity
I say,
Eaten for lunch by the War Gods.
We pretend we are helping to make things OK.
Save the Iraqis,
Build democracy in the middle-east.
How noble. How stupid.
The Sunni hates, the Shiite who hates the Alawite,
who hates the Wahabbi, who hates the Suffi
And all hate one another and themselves but all
hate the infidel.
("The enemy of my enemy is my friend".)
Welcome to Hell.
We ignore the poverty, the disease, the hopelessness
at home.
And elsewhere.
Thank God for Xmas
We let the good feelings come.

As we contemplate our generosities
We feel them in our groin.
It has sexual connotations.
Gift giving.
Our personal generosities
We feel important with our donations.
We become aroused
We pat ourselves on the back.
We massage our privates
We give testimonials to the givers,
To the takers and to the destroyers
Of life.
Can I kiss your ass Mr. President.
No?
Then what else may I kiss?
We honor the despicable and they
Run for office.
We elect them.
We worship our Gods in vain, I think.
But all is vanities, and all is lost.
Eventually, everything dies or is killed or mutilated,
Eventually! the spirt dies, our loved ones disappear.
Especially the innocent, especially the children,
Until they cannot be recognized
As children
Because they grow up to be the damned
And carry on the carnage.
Sing praises to the Lord of Entropy.
But, I live in hope.
Honest, cross my heart
And hope to die.

Your Sweet Caress

I like being near you
I like being by your side
It makes me feel just
Wonderful,
Way down deep, inside.
I don't know what your
Magic is.
I can't figure it all out.
But that it's there,
I have not a single doubt
I think about you always
Morning, noon and night
It kind of drives me crazy
When you are out of sight
So hold me close
Beloved,
It's what we have to share
It makes these moments right.
And without them I'd despair
It seems like when you're away
I live in empty space
There is nothing that can console me
Until I feel your warm embrace.
I know that if you ever leave me
I would die of loneliness
I would die of loneliness
Without your sweet caress.

A Curse on Me

Wicked woman,
Have you put a curse on me?
If not
Then what is the cause of my misery,
Daughter of Eve
Conniving what new infamy?
It seems that the moment my eyes fell on you
I've been living in a lover's hell
For the want of you.
Damn it, smell the smoke,
I'm burning to death
Is this not hell's own breath.
I can't breathe, I'll surely choke
On my own agonies
Until I expire,
Hopefully between your knees
Have mercy, woman of Sodom.
You're driving me crazy rib of Adom.
I'll die on my sword
Or end my days on a mental ward.
Killing my self for this wanton desire,
Suffering in this burning pyre,
Oh, what a wretched way to pass
What do you mean eternal virgin
I'm crass?
I'm the heart of innocence.
Ask my mother.
I wish I could say the same for you.

Trouble's Comin Your Way

Hey Buddy!
I can see trouble a comin your way
And you can't hide,
No matter how hard you try to pray
Trouble ain't goin go away,
No, trouble ain't gonna go away
I repeat
There's big trouble comin up your way
Are you listenin, Squirt
I require your complete attention
So be prepared for this big alert.
Do you hear me?
Look at me and say
You understand my words.
Keep your ears open
And your pea size brain, focused.
I repeat again, for penetration purposes.
And none of your sass.
Trouble is gonna bug you brother
Real bad!
I mean, it will bite you severely on the ass
And bug spray won't do no good
To stem the blood flow
Or the tears
That is gonna grow
Like a river in your eyes
What the hell you mean
"You don't care?"

I dislike punk wise guys.
I am trying to save your sorry ass.
Ca' bish? Senor Jackass.
They say you ain't tough enuff
To withstand the guff.
You are about to receive
So be prepared, brother
And don't annoy your poor ole mother
With your tales of woe
Cause she can't help you.
Now, I've got go
No more prophesizing for me
My crystal ball has gotten cloudy
Must be the wind bringin on the rain
And you know that rhymes with pain.

Into the Darkness

Into the darkness softly,
Be not afraid to go,
It is from whence you came,
In the Beginning.
To which you will return,
At the end.
It is not hostile there.
It is a place of comfort.
The sounds are melodious there,
It is said.
It is serene, comforting.
It is place of kindness,
Of quietness and gentleness.
It is the nest your mother
Prepared for you long ago.
Even before you were born
Even before she was born
Knowing that you would return,
To her.
As her mother did for her.
She will embrace you,
Your ancestors will receive you
With loving arms.
Do not fight the darkness.
It is our destiny.
All.
Rejoice.

A Stranger from Hell

But you said you didn't love me
You said that you didn't care
It was all over, you said
Then came that gruesome stare
I should go away is what you said
You were very emphatic, and
Didn't pull a punch
I begged and pleaded
It was like you had had me for your lunch.
You said I wasn't needed
You said, I shouldn't cry,
That you had upped and found another guy
You said, "don't give me any static"
"Just go away".
You were very cruel on that wretched day.
Just go away is what you said
Go away! Go away!, and
I knew that I was dead,
It was excruciating pain just
Pounding in my head
I didn't believe it was you talking.
Not the one, I loved.
Now you were a stranger
A stranger from hell
I never saw that side of you before
Maybe I did, but it was one I chose to ignore,
The stranger from hell
I cringed and cried
And,
I knew my heart would break

But I took your advice and
I went away,
To get well
And break the spell
Of the stranger from hell
And then, I found this some one
A special love one
Or maybe he/she found me.
It broke the curse and I was free
I don't remember exactly when
But, it's been great since then
Not as passionate as it was with you
But getting over you was rough
And I'm not that tough
Not anymore.
It was the fabric of my life you tore
I hold back now,
Can you blame me?
When you shamed me
I don't give everything away
Like when you held sway
I'm just protecting myself.
Can you blame me?
You tell me now,
This other guy was a big mistake
A fake
And you want me back.
No thanks, I'll pass.
I don't want the stranger from hell.

Graduation

It's time to leave the nest
Do not hesitate,
Fears thicken on second thoughts
Lift your wings, higher still
Now leap forward, flapping furiously
Boldly and confidently.

Sweep above the horizon into the limitless sky
See the fantastic vistas
The extravagant loves
The extraordinary adventures awaiting.

Do not look back,
Some have already crashed
They will be forgotten
Others glide into quite obscurity
But not you nor I.

I Dreamed Away the Years

I've dreamed away the years before
In another time and place.
I've drifted in an aimless way
From coast to coast
And space to space.
I've tried to settle down and find a place
To lay my head
There is no spot for me, I guess,
Until I'm dead, until I'm dead
I've married several times before and
Bedded quite a few
I've got couple kids somewhere and
There are some I never knew
I'm not a perfect guy for sure
I've conned the crowd and rolled the drunk
I've spilled the wine and smoked some junk
My mother's all I got a home
But I've been away for years
I've thought about goin back,
I couldn't stand the tears.
I figure no one really cares
So what the hell's the use
I lived my life and I'll die my death
There ain't much else to choose.

Viva

They don't sleep together anymore
I saw his mattress on the floor
The spread and sheets were disarrayed
Her pad in another room was laid
His clothes were strewn across the rug
I gave my heart a mournful tug
Because I remember when first they wed
They could not wait to get to bed
Their passion shamed them not at all
We smiled and smirked as I recall
For proud and boastful there he stood
To whip the world, we bet he could
And on her mouth a wanton pout
It was just enough to make you shout
We hoped the first would be a boy
They laughed and smiled just filled with joy
And off they sped to nuptials lair
Where she had swore his weight to bear
There marriage was not a happy lesson
She bore five girls in quick succession
But he did not seem to have the grit
To make a living and do his bit
So they lived like welfared poor
Their home was never clean for sure
The kitchenware was stored in piles
The bathroom covered with dirty tiles
Then, she got fed up and refused to play
And he decided he would stray
To save, he said, his dignity and pride
He bragged he drank and other women tried

The girls grew up and eventually left home
They do on occasion phone

He eventually just upped and died
And no one cried
No one cried at all
Then she remarried.

Let The Juices Flow

In Memory of English Poet Robert Herrick

Let the juices flow
Why put on the widow's cap and
Bank the fires low?
Why close the grate?
Let all despair dissipate
Before it becomes too late
To burn passion's sweet desire
With God's own fruitful fire.
Let the Lord's love preside
Unfettered and un-denied
By the ranting of the orthodox
That would forever shutter youth's
Pleasure shaft and velvet box
And brutishly consign the Lord's sweet lust
And its pregnant blessings
To one's own mortal dust.
Yes, heaven forefend
The sod's wet embrace is life's cruel end.
So what madness, then is this
In which you must not persist.
No nun's garb for thee
God forbids it.
Let love's sugary juices run free
Now Go! Seek a lover everywhere,
Before you dissolve into atoms of despair
And I am called to make repair.

Genesis

We are creatures of the deep, some say
Born in a briny seep, some way
A soup in which combined certain atoms,
You'll find
Floating even now in outer space.
These ions were refined into creatures called
mankind
More precisely into molecules such as you and I
Now much of this guess,
For if you examine this sorry mess
You will probably conclude
At the cost of being rude
That mom and dad have lied
About the origins of your hide
Thus deserving patricide.

Sex

Sex in the morn
Do not scorn
Sex at noon
None to soon
Sex all night
Pure delight
Sex all day
Hip, Hip Hurray.

Stoned

Intergalactic spaced out assholes
Sucking prune pits to the rhythmic
Whine of the cosmic snake
Hearken to the brain beats
Whipping nasal snot from the upper lip
Waterbeds, watery eyes, self-lies
In the incremental nothingness of the
Big Stone.
I can't find where fug was, cause he
Wasn't where he was.

The Virgin

Where am I going now?
Into your innermost sanctum
To savor your innocence
Long dicked I
To touch those walls
No other man has touched.
Perhaps a delusion,
Then on to Carthage and to Babylon
For the really big squirm
Images of myself to build
In your empty room
I am forever the victim of the big swell.

Passion

Shall I tell her that I love her
Shall I tell that I care
Shall I tell that I want her
Do I, do I dare

Will she treat with derision?
Will she mock me with her scorn?
Will she deny me my obsession?
Make me sorry I was born

Then I'll screw on the ceiling
I'll screw on the floor
I try to keep her reeling
Screaming, lover give me more

Will she forgive my passion?
Will she forgive my lust?
Respond with similar emotion?
Good lord, I know she must.

Her beauty is her treasure
Her smile warm, sincere
A woman without measure
A flower, without peer.

For Pleasure's Sake

Let me slip betwixt your lips
In undulating dips
Trowel in hand I glide
Pushing curly hairs aside
Soft sucking sounds we'll make
All for pleasure's sake
In each variety
Finding fluid harmony
Moving both together in syncopated measure
We never seem to tire
Though your nest is wet with fire
My scepter brightly glows
As we gyrate in the throes
Impassioned souls to free
In our orgiastic spree.

Ill Wind

You can tell it to the north wind
You can tell it to the sea
You can tell it to the moon and stars
Cause it cuts no ice with me
You said it once to often
And I proved it was a lie
To make me do your bidding
But now I'd rather die

You can humiliate a person
Then drag them in the dirt
It's a kind of sickness maybe
Looking for a hurt.

But time is your own enemy
And even love wears out
So now your words ring false
No matter how you shout

Yes, you have lost your so called beauty
Your looks have begun to fade
Those crows feet don't add glamour
To what you have to trade

Cruelty has no master, it trips from tongue to
tongue
Whatever sounds you hear from me my love
Are from the bell that you first rung.

Red Lightening

Don't say you ever loved before
Unless you loved with me
I've got a special style kid
The likes you won't believe
It starts a little slow at first
And then it gains some speed
Before you know it lass
The lights begin to weave
Crazy patterns on the ceiling glass
That's when you know
You're in trouble sweets
Cause the devil's got you by the ass

I'm the devil love, and the devil does it right
He puts it in your own silk box
And screws the lid down tight
You can squirm and turn, yell or shout
And try and get away
But the devil has you in his clutch
He's got the final say

Now climb aboard my lighting rod
And grab me with your knees
Then squeeze it with your special parts
I promise not to wheeze

We'll ride this donkey into town
And never slacken pace
And finish up our interlude
Screwing face to face.

Mr. Lucky

Your good fortune rankles me
It gets beneath my skin
Whatever you seem to do
You always seem to win

I buy a dozen lotteries
You buy only one
Naturally, the lottery you buy
Is the lottery that's won

I violate a litter law and wind up
Locked in jail
You violate the whole damn book
They pin a medal on your tail

We play a round of poker
A game I know so well
You win each and every hand
While my luck goes straight to hell

I make a small financial error
End up deep in debt
You make the same damn mistake
Like a diamond, you are set.

The odds just seem to go your way
No matter what the game.
For me it just the opposite,
I always come up lame.

They say that there is some justice there
Waiting in the wings.
I pray the posse says,
That you're the guy who swings.

Monkey Business

The monkey crossed its leg
And kissed its banana on the ass
The banana smiled sweetly
While the monkey polished brass
The banana unperturbed
Yellowed up to brown
Unzipped its skin
And dropped it to the ground
Then the monkey skidded to a halt
And mumbled “Hey hick, Ich liebe dich”
The banana blushed to red
And slipped it out of sight
Singing to itself,
“Don’t do it lest you do it right”

Our Relationship

What happened to our relationship?
It started out so well
Then for some peculiar reason
It began to have that telltale lift
Of things gone all adrift
So, let's get out into the open
And try.....
To nail it like it was one big lie,
Now!
If you really cared for me
Way down deep that is
You wouldn't say the things
You do,
Because they cut me to the quick
And when you say them like you do
They can make a body sick
Instead you should say loving things
Like how I love to smell your hair
Or my dearest darling love
I always adore the clothes you wear
Not because you look so winsome
But because my love, I find you in some
Otherwise, you're one big nag
Acting like an empty bag.
Now!
I've given you an ultimatum
Please find some loving words, with,
The mindset that can create them.
There is no point in hurting one another
No point at all... as far as I can judge.

So try to give those loving words,
A very healthy loving nudge.
Otherwise, my darling dear
We're headed for the courts
Where, I guarantee you sweet pea
I'll get a loving divorce decree.

I Surrender

The nights are cold even though it's summer
The days are worse and it's a bummer
This pain and sorrow have got to end.
So
Why don't you just go away
You've got it all
Everything I own
There is nothing more for me to pawn
Except the midnight and the dawn
I just want to be alone
Now go and have yourself a ball
No, be my guest have two
That should more than satisfy
The nasty greed in you
I'm through with all this wrangling
And legal crap and senseless
Tangling
You've played me for a dummy
And I admit that you have won
This war;
You bet I'm sore
I hate to lose and take the rap
But I surrender.
Now go away
Enjoy your victory, and have your fun
I want nothing more than
Peace of mind and heart
And;
A brand new start
A place to begin again

To win again
Some self respect
Don't phone, never
I don't want to hear your voice,
Or your name, ever
I hope you feel the same.
So just go away and keep on going
I've lost and you've won.
I surrender.

A Gentleman's Proposal

This evening has been so delightful and
Our conversation so intelligent and
Insightful.
That I am convinced we have met in a past life
Or even two
There is something so familiar and charming
about the person who is you,
I am sure we were not just a distant he and she
But coupled, intimately
In this other time and place,
I hope, you find this no disgrace
Perhaps it was as husband and wife,
That you and I were spliced
in this other life.
No!, No! I am certain, it was as lovors.
Nothing is more appealing than this romantic
tie that history favors
For a lovor is very core of friendship;
Even more so than kinship, in my opinion
It makes a liaison more enduring
Than unhappy life with a wife and family
Don't you agree?
I see you nodding your head but alas in the wrong
direction
I hope that is not a suggestion
That I mean nothing to you, nothing at all?
An idea that I would have good reason to appall,
Or that you could not fancy me as lovor.
A wretched thought, that both my dear
ancestors and I would certainly abhor.

I do not sense this hostile sentiment emanating from you
That is not the message you are sending
And, I assure you that I am not pretending
When I state without dispute, we were once related...
Somehow,
Tethered in another time and space,
I allow.
I believe my analysis is correct and factual and
And since all relationships are socially contractual.
I need strong words from you
Something very positive, something
We could both deem dispositive
of this concern.
I would despair believing that I am alone,
in this romantic endeavor.
It would embarrass me with my friends forever,
If you sought to disagree with me;
Publicly,
It would sound as if I had concocted an insane notion,
Sprung from an alcoholic potion, that I had imbibed, this evening .
Without your full support,
It might be taken that I have lied, about this evening
I pray again that I have your unconditional rapport.
Yes, it matters,

Otherwise it leaves my solid reputation in tatters.
While, I do not suggest you make foolish declarations
Or try to describe our present or future relations, without instructions from me.
You see, I have family.
And must be careful not to offend, its members on either end.
Regrettably, I find your silence provoking
And not exactly evoking of further discourse
Or any other form of gratifying intercourse.
So please,
Say something, if only to appease,
Unfortunately, if you find yourself reluctant
And believe sincerely that you can't
Although I must sadly disapprove
There is one conclusion that
I will not remove, from our evening's chat.
I insist that I'm heels over head in love with you.

Next Door

Why did I kiss you then?
I just got this crazy notion when
I heard this buzz go off in my foolish head
It was a sudden impulse,
Yes, a most peculiar impulse
The kind of impulse that I dread
An impulse that can lead one to a marriage bed
I recall that all I did was to lean forward
Just to kiss you on your curly top
When we discovered that our lips had locked
The coupling was so electrifying,
I was truly shocked,
Your eyes glistened madly in the dark
They had this sexy shimmer and they sparked
With that lethal "come hither look."
My hands trembled and my legs shook
We kissed once more, passionately
I could not imagine what fate had in store
My world was swirling all around
For I knew that at last I had found
The woman I had been yearning for
Amazingly, she had been living, right next door
Yet, how could I have been so blind,
When it was she that I had been trying so
desperately to find.
Tell me beloved, do you think your husband will
mind?

The Lesson

The weather never bothered me
The rain the snow, the bitter cold or
The blinding heat,
Are something I could take in stride
As long as you were by my side
Woman, how I loved you
When you first became my bride
But you aren't here; not any more
So now, it's everything that I ignore
The sun, the moon, the stars, the sky
I keep on asking for the reasons why;
You split and did not even say good bye
I tried to give you the very best I could;
Just ask around
I worshiped the very ground
On which you stood
The guys would grow crazy when I described
Your looks
Some accused me of stealing words from
Romantic books
But I swore that everything I said was true
Maybe that's the reason; I lost you.
Maybe it was some hungry guy
That wanted some of my sweet cherry pie
That I described for him, so well.
If that's the case,
Then both of you can burn in Hell.

The Seadog

I like a rainy day
When the skies are brownish gray
And the raindrops play a steady drumbeat
On my deck
I stretch out in my bunk
Getting mellow, not quite drunk
While anchored in a secret cove
Itself a kind of treasure trove
Here I reminisce the passing hour
In the confines of my private bower
Of making love to tawny mermaids
Mermaids not exactly from the sea
While the ocean pitched and tore
At my vessel and the shore
Adding to the passion and the score
Of that young sea dog that was me.

But now I'm old and gray
Long in the tooth you might say.
And obliged to confess a sorrow
There is no gladness in tomorrow
For the only one at home is me
Yes, the only one at home is me.
Maybe now it's time to die
Done in by swollen sea and yellow sky
While the wild wind and frothy wave
Speed me to a salty grave
For there's no joy to be alone
To hear the ocean moan
When the only one at home is me.

Pope John XXIII

Father Giovanni have they heard you
Down through the centuries
To the time of the hot pincers and the torture rack
Have they heard you to the time of Torequemada,
To the beginnings on the cross
Have they heard you above the raucous chorus
Seeking a lost God in the milky way
Have they heard you today
To the point of credulity and compromise
I think not.
They have heard only their economic self-
interests,
Their historical prejudices,
Their self-consuming hatreds
Yet above the din of their voices
I have heard you Father Giovanni down through
the ages
Calling for reason, for compassion and forgiveness
In the shrieks of the sacked and raped villages of
my ancestors,
In the agonizing wails muted in the burning pyres
of the death camps
In the sweet and innocent voices of our children
I have heard you and felt you caress my soul.

The Big Snore

I hate it when you snore
You make this awesome roar
It sounds just like a war
It penetrates the door
It vibrates through the floor
It destroys my inner core
I don't want to hear it anymore
I cover up my ears
I try to control my tears
I grab a pair of shears
Judge, I'll make my plea
Innocent by reason of insanity

A Weekend at the Shore

We went to the seashore,
My friend, my son and I
In September.
The day was beautiful, tranquil,
The temperature was in the eighties.
A day when your heart sang.
You were reborn.
There was a sign,
It read:
"No Dogs Allowed on the Boardwalk or Beach
Between May 1 and Oct 1."
It was well intended,
Visitors don't care to step or lie down in
Dog Doo.
I don't.
I don't like unpleasant memories
With this reading,
I recalled a painful weekend.
Many, many years ago.
A bitter memory,
There was another sign.
A nasty sign
The word dog was there.
The four of us.
Vinnie Agresti, Mike Del Pomo Frankie Scalera
and myself.
Planned a weekend at the shore.
We were young and innocent.
We had saved for this event.
Off we sped,

To a small nondescript hotel in Belmar NJ
A proud group of virgin comrades.
Hoping, for the improbable:
To meet some young ladies
Eager to donate their virginity to a good cause.
Even a willing older woman would do.
We were all nervously awaiting that big moment.
That would make men of us all.
We left the hotel and I noticed
A sign on the hotel lawn that read:
"No Dogs or Jews Allowed"
I was stunned,
I don't know whether the other guys saw it.
If they did, they pretended they didn't
I pretended I didn't.
I was the only Jew.
In case you wondered.
The owner of the hotel pretended it wasn't there.
He took our money.
I was humiliated by the sign.
The weekend was a washout for me.
I found it especially bitter because the word,
Dogs preceded the word Jews.
For years, the sign haunted me.
If you wanted to bring your dog
Or a Jew to the beach or boardwalk.
To take a dump in Belmar. NJ
I wouldn't have said a word.
The world has changed somewhat since then.
The other guys are dead.

But, I would still like my revenge.
If I could remember where the hotel was,
I would have my dog make on the lawn.
At night, of course.
I am a Jewish gentlemen, now.
Received in the best hotels.
Haunted by memories.

Don't Please Call

When, I die, please don't cry,
I leave no forwarding address
I'm sure, you'll try,
Perhaps,
Try to guess
To what venue of the afterlife,
I'll fly
Hopefully, without success.
I don't wish to be annoyed
By your foolish quest.
Therefore,
May I suggest,
That you get on with your life.
No need to pry into mine.
I'll be fine
No, I won't have a cell phone.
Even if I did, I'd prefer silence
And a place to rest
That is how they bury you
Nowadays.
So don't be a pest
I intend to keep my whereabouts,
A mystery, unknown
Plainly, this old wretch has flown
Do I sense annoyance on your part?
Too bad, bye, bye.
Rest assured,
I won't try to contact you either,
Busybody.

Hanging Tough

I'm so damn tired of hanging tough.
Damn tired of playing life in the rough,
I want to be free
Play life on an endless green
Where life is carefree and serene
No sand traps there
Just a clean hit to the pin,
With win following win.
Scoring a big 67
Before I even get to heaven.
I know it's not to be.
There is always one more responsibility.
One more pile of manure.
To be shoveled as we endure.
I guess, I must like the suffering,
The tensions and the endless buffeting.
Otherwise, I swear, I'd chuck it all
And head for the hills
Without my bucket of pills.
Maybe there, I can live tall
High wide and handsome,
For this I'd gladly pay a king's ransom
Not to be, you say?
Hey! FU
Tomorrow's another day
And I got an exit plan.

Humankind or Unkind

So much happening in this world
Most choose not to understand or to ignore.
Hordes at each other's throat
Some scream for peace
And others declare for war.
World economies are out of sorts,
Our own headed for the dumps.
Nations overwhelmed by insidious diseases,
Fratricidal war
Destabilizing the world.
Many millions extremely rich
Yet billions upon billions are destitute.
Savvy crooks suffer no punishment.
Others become their scapegoats.
For justice is blind and cruel.
The federal system is a dirty joke.
Most will never shine or blossom in the sun.
Enjoy the blessings and fruits of the world.
They blow themselves up, hoping for a better afterlife.
Politicians and judges and high-ranking clergy
Violate their oaths with impunity.
They go unpunished and are venerated.
Weapons of mass destruction are waiting to be released.
All kinds of natural calamities are destined for earthlings.

Hurricanes, earthquakes, floods, droughts, tsunamis, diseases, volcanic eruptions, climatic catastrophes, asteroids and comets crashing into planet earth wiping out all living creatures.
Against such forces we are powerless.
Why can't we work together, love one another , help one another before it is too late?
Because most of us are completely mad with our own self importance.
Perhaps, it is already too late.

Make Me a Salad

You said make me a salad,
Without thinking, I said OK.
A verbal reflex,
Wanting to please.
I figured that there could be a big payoff,
For small favors.
I won't say that I am horny,
But I figure.
That one good turn,
Deserves another good turn.
Reciprocity, so to speak.
A bit of a platitude to be sure.
But the world feeds on platitudes.
Like "Save the World for Democracy,
American for the Americans.
Our Nation Right or Wrong!"
So what does a bit of scheming matter,
If it intends to get a woman into bed
And pleasure her.
The world could disappear tomorrow.
Why leave her with regrets.

Regrets

Once I had a friend
His name was Bud.
Bud had everything, intelligence,
Good looks, great personality,
A pleasant disposition and cancer.
He was then thirty-five years old.
We were in business together
When he announced he was going
To die.
His first wife divorced him.
He quit our business and
Went to live on Long Island.
There,
He obtained a Real Estate License
And a new wife.
One day Bud called me and said he was very sick.
He asked me to attend his birthday party.
He also said he had something very
Important to tell me.
It was the fall of the year.
I said that I would attend.
I did not.
I was afraid of death then.
I had seen too much of it.
I had been surrounded by it.
I hated it.
It was so damn uncompromising.
It snuffed out young lives with an appetite
That was grotesque and malevolent.
Bud died shortly after his birthday

I attended his funeral.
It was at St. John The Divine in NYC.
His new wife was rich.
She wanted to prove her love,
So she gave him a splendid funeral.
All these years, I regretted not attending Bud's birthday party.
I did not forgive myself.
Now,
I make it my business to see sick friends.
During the passing years,
I have seen and tasted death many times.
I know that Mr. Skeletor will come for me,
I hope I have the courage to face him
And spit him in the eye.
Maybe, if I see Bud again,
He will tell me what was so important.

Road Kill

On Route 280 to the Garden State Parkway
I caught sight of
A kitten, crushed to death on that
Mindless River of Steel
It's neck wrapped in a blue collar
Did I also see or imagine a pink ribbon?
The mind plays tricks,
We are apt to believe anything,
In our world of the irrational.
I see a child mourning the loss of
Her kitty cat, when it jumped from the car
Or was it simply hurled there
As so much offal?
Morbid thoughts of road kill
Do you eat road kill?
Ten Thousand miles away
On the highways of Baghdad
A blazing unarmored Humvee,
The acrid smell of burning flesh,
Road bomb, and more road kill.
Four GIs slaughtered there,
Tossed into harms way, willy nilly, to
Satisfy a mad man's dream?
Perhaps!
While at home the family mourns
The loss of its sons and daughters
For whom and for what,
That Haliburton may profit handsomely
While it devours road kill.

So the Imperial Saudis may harvest their oil
revenues
Before their tyranny implodes?

Listen,
Their Wahabi cousins spew
Hatred of the infidel.
There, Al Qaeda recruits its warriors
There our enemies reside.
We are the infidel.
But,
I do not identify with
The infidel tin soldier, is he a Saudi partner?
Playing Mars, our master fiddles in Washington
pretending he has a plan
To democratize the Middle East
While creating road kill.
He could have started with Saudi Arabia
from whence cometh
Al Qaeda.
This weekend warrior, gone AWOL,
A Commander and Chief without
Credentials
I would like to laugh, at the image;
I dare not.
The families must believe their road kills
Were not in vain.

Something to Eat

When I think of something to eat,
I think of my mother's chicken soup.
It was the only thing she couldn't burn.
I can still smell it simmering in the pot.
It had a nurturing and heady aroma.
When I was in the infantry and on the march,
Food was often scarce or inedible,
Her chicken soup was a recurrent dream.
I saw myself walking into her kitchen and shouting
"Hi, mom, I'm home, what's for dinner?"
I smelled the soup and heard it
Gurgling cheerfully in the pot.
I walked over to the pot and lifted the cover,
I breathed in deeply, anticipating the
Heavenly rush with the first tablespoon.
At that very moment, some Son of a Bitch
Kicked my boot and whispered hoarsely,
"Get up, we're movin out."
I hated that bastard.
He was the enemy.

The Homecoming Queen

They were going to have a birthday party for her
Or was it a homecoming?
She was going home
To the great mystery of life and death.
To the ultimate truth, the home of homes.
Those who knew her felt angry and very sad.
The sadness, because she had much to live for.
And anger comes with the feeling of helplessness
She was too young to pass over the divide.
“Not yet!” they all chorused with her.
But, thus it had been decreed.
She tried to escape the sentence,
Neither the X-rays nor the chemo prevailed.
There was no cure to be found,
The forces of entropy were allied against her
In her hologram,
Her past, present and future co existed,
In this nether world,
All was predetermined.
The beginning, the end and the in between.
They were all there.
The metastases had spread first to her eye,
Then to her entire brain.
She tried to smile.

The Aftermath

With the collapse of the WTC,
Came this thick layer of impenetrable dust.
Rising up with the agony of a nation
A nation that had not felt the sting of war
On its own turf for over hundred years.
Came this a poisonous mix of building materials,
Flesh, blood and asbestos released from its captivity.
The detritus of a 20th century civilization.
That had known innumerable wars
In its anguished history.
Now a nation was confronted with
A declaration of War.
From unknowns?
Conveyed clearly
With this ground up mess of fine corrosive particulates.
Who had dared to challenge this supreme nuclear power?
Who?
What came with this disintegration was a blood lust
nurtured in the bowels
Of a nation gone bonkers.
A blood lust that spread its miasma of revenge
Over the entire world,
Without regard to individual guilt or innocence?
Exacting an appalling penalty from those who had
nothing to do
With the original crime or sin.
It said to the remotest hamlet in the world:
Do not ever believe that you are invulnerable.
Do not dare to believe that you are free from attack.
Never again!

The 3000 plus who perished in the attack were not the last to know the sting of death.
The Afgan and Iraq wars aside.
To add horror to insult,
The Queen of Air Quality in Washington DC
Announced that the dust was safe and breathable,
A obvious misstatement of reality.
The dust was caustic and cancerous.
The utterance was made
Without the slightest evidence of truth .
She offered deceit and callous indifference.
This unholy pawn vomiting murderous lies from the black corridors
Of our nation's capitol.
Perhaps the workers should have known better?
Perhaps not.
But their nation's government had said it was safe
There was no dispute.
No quibble from any other source.
The good Samaritans who had rushed to ground zero,
To extract living victims from the catastrophe.
Were caught up in the frenzy of the moment.
In the chaotic mixture of broken glass, steel and concrete,
Of flesh and bones and blood to save, if possible
Those buried alive in the senseless slaughter.
Becoming themselves victims of a religion gone mad
From its own compulsive contradictions.
These good Samaritans had volunteered without constraint,
Without regard for their own bodies.

These good Samaritans had willingly sucked in this lethal mixture
Breathing the muck so deeply into their being,
To become an integral part of their bodies,
Their worst nightmares.
Now they are suffering living death;
Many cannot breathe or eat.
Their sinuses bleed as they gasp for air.
Washington has nothing to say.
The State of New York has nothing to say.
The City of New York has nothing to say.
No one seems to care.
The dead are gone.
The QB denies her culpability but we know better.
What about the 20,0000 wounded living? You ask
Why, F em!
Let's erect a memorial instead.
To the big dicks in DC, especially the dumb CC.
Who has abdicated his responsibilities.
He deserves it in his ground zero.

The Bibliophile

(A Soliloquy With Chorus)

I have this wild thought
That I cannot contain.
For it is what I alone have wrought
I will not hear criticism of it,
Nor should there be any,
If implemented, it will make my present stay on this planet glorious.
Perhaps, even a bit notorious.
What is it?, you ask.
Simply put, when I die, I wish to be buried in a bookstore.
Wait, I know that the concept is new for you.
But give it a moment, I implore
You see; I have always loved the bookstore.
It is a magnet for me, the ultimate attraction for me.
My feelings, I confess, are somewhat sinful,
Yet, I will never apologize for my passion.
It is one of utter fascination with the private parts, so to speak, of a bookstore.
Its shelves of books, its tapes, CDs, and magazines;
Its rest rooms and so much more.
And then viola, there are books at a discount.
I love books at a discount.
Books, for me, are immortal.
They open this and that and most every portal.
I appreciate the tremendous effort it requires to Write one and certainly, to type one.
The idea of being buried in a bookstore is not so
Outlandish as it may appear at first blush,
But first, let me prove my point and ask what are coffins made from?

Now take your time.... and do not rush.
And then, consider, if you will,
What are books made from?
Ah!, now you see the woodsy part of this drill
Can you think of a more practical and rational use
of old books, used books, even magazines, and
pornographic comic books?
And where, may I ask, can you find these items
without travail?
Why in a bookstore and hopefully on sale.
N'est ce pas?
I want to be buried in a box made from expired volumes
of Encyclopedia Britannica.
To which I will add, as leavening, Scientific American
and Popular Mechanica.
Customers having heard of my unique interment
Will, upon announcement, want to visit the bookstore
that hosts such an illustrious exhibit on display.
It may even start a fad, Quien sabe!
It certainly will be good for business,
You shall see!,
For, it is not as odd as it may seem,
This notion of a bookstore mausoleum.
Yes, I shall patent the idea
And leave the royalties to my posterity.
Now, if I can persuade Barnes and Noble or Borders to
entertain such an idea while I am still alive,
The memory of my current stay on earth then shall
happily survive.
Unless of course, if I can persuade them to sell my first
book of poetry, when written.
Honestly, what's your opinion?

The Koan

The Koan
Is Zen Buddhist.
Is a parable or
A contradiction, a paradox
Or an itch?
Scalp or groin,
Maybe anal.
It's supposed to teach something.
That is was or was not.
Did you miss it?
Because,
You didn't see it
Or heard it.
It is not supposed to make you feel
Stupid,
Or humble,
Or simple
Or smug,
Or great,
Or giggly if you got it
Or didn't
What are we discussing anyway?
You weren't listening.
I was so!
The Koan.
It's the name of a Jewish Delicatessen,
On the west side of Manhattan.
Serves a great pastrami sandwich
What?
You never ate there?
You don't eat meat!

The Message

Sometimes the message comes from the bright corners of my mind.
Sometimes the message comes from the dark side.
Sometimes the message is soft and soulful full of tenderness and love
Sometimes the message is mean and angry like a tornado
A tornado ready and eager to tear the head off those bastards
Who would send young men to their death
And visit terror on women and children.
For their misbegotten legacies.
How and when the inspiration will happen,
I have no clue,
When the message will come, it will come.
Sometimes, I try to force the sometimes and sometimes it works.
Then again, I can hit a dry period when nothing happens.
I go blank, as if my mind had deserted me.
Not a word, not a sound not a frisson of inspiration will come.
Then I know I have to sit and wait.
I have learned to wait patiently.
It or they will come when it or they will come
Sometimes as a word, or a phrase, or as a vision.
It will come and I will hear it and perhaps even see it.

It will say write me down and hurry otherwise you will lose me.
Often, I do lose the me.
This loss comes with a passing regret but I do not mourn.
I have no time to mourn about a missed poem
when there so much else to mourn.
And I prefer to sing the songs of my youth
And paint the bright colors of the universe
That I am privileged to see.

The Sun

I hold nothing inviolate
Praying that you will become upset
With this contentious view
Of genesis
That today, tomorrow even yesterday
Are nothing more than beams of light
A friend or nemesis
From our Sun, the God of sight,
Presenting infinite possibilities,
Imaginings
To everything that's seen or been
Or we can ever hope to seize.
As transitory surfers here.
Riding waves or particles of mortal fear,
Until that ride becomes a mortal crime
And then we pay our debt;
Forfeiting our earthly time.
And prayerfully, without regret.
Noting, that what we are or were
Or wished to be
Was but an illusion of this light and
Nuanced shade
By our heaven's painter laid.
And that what we think we know,
Was just another corollary
Of "To be or not to be."

It is this rule of light and shade
Into whose shadows,
All of us will one day fade,
That declares unequivocally
"It is up to us,
How we spend our illusory time.
In pursuit of yours and mine.
Or in something far more sublime.
Until we hear, our herald's beckoning cry,
Lights out!"

Small Treasures

I hope, when I have slipped out of sight,
You will find amid the memories shared
Recollections of loving hours
With luminous bodies paired

A fragment of a poem, a horse,
A picture painted, a porcelain cow,
Some one thing that will delight you,
I'll allow.

I pray, these mementoes of great times,
Will fill you with pleasant recall
Where you will find insights,
Into the why and wonder of it all.

A romantic dalliance that saw,
Spring mixed with winter's waning hour
Knowing there was something there,
That spring and love could flower.

When all of this has passed
Perhaps what we can surmise
That this world is a madman's invention
Of surprise upon surprise.

A hologram, where past, present, and future merge;
with infinite strings
And Love catches all,
Within its embracing wings.

I Remember a Song

I remember a song that I sang
Long ago on forced marches.
The words go:
"You are my sunshine
My only sunshine,
You make me happy
When skies are gray."

I won't say now that
You are my only sunshine.
There are others,
But,
You do illuminate my heart, my soul and my mind.
The quintessential me,
Whoever, I am.

I love you beyond my understanding.
And this love does not require an external
Sunshine or even a rationale.
The fire comes from my own atomic furnace
Burning passionately within me.
Who says love is rational!
I am now a cinder of the original me.
What do mean you wish to use me in your barbeque?
This is love poetry, lady.
I am not for frying, broiling perhaps.

Bumper Stickers

I read bumper stickers.
I am not ashamed that I do.
I don't think it violates the
Patriot Act, yet.
It may, one day.
All our readings may violate
The Patriot Act.
Bumper stickers may become Obsolete.
An American tragedy in the offing?
You ask.
Maybe, but don't despair.
We will be able to read their equivalent
On the underground internet, maybe.
I have gotten a lot of knowledge From bumper
stickers, in the past
Luckily and selfishly, I am not worried
About a police state.
I have often said "AFTER ME THE DELUGE. "
Not original, but appropriate.
I have not seen that bit of wisdom
On a bumper sticker, yet.
I know for instance that there is not
Enough time to do all the women in the world.
SO MANY WOMEN SO LITTLE TIME.
I have learned that THE ONE WHO DIES WITH
THE MOST TOYS WINS.
From bumper stickers I was taught
That we have the right to vote
For some liar and potential spendthrift to a
responsible seat in our government.

It leaves me with a warm feeling knowing
That I can quickly scan a bumper sticker
And harvest so much knowledge so quickly
If you have a problem with this effort,
I am offering a three week course
With college credits for $3,000. Entitled:
How To Read Bumper Stickers Quickly And Safely
That's a $1,000 per week for those of you
Who are challenged mathematically as well.

Love Poetry

This odd-ball book of love poetry,
That I have been reading,
With its wide range of attitudes,
Inspires me to write my own.
I should be an expert by now.
But am I, are you?
My attitude is simple.
I like love expressed physically and verbally,
With passion.
Repeat please, "I love you."
Perhaps the phrase sounds hollow.
Simplistic, lacking in subtlety even grace,
Not unlike a burp or its bottom echo,
Exploding inappropriately?
At some fancy dinner party,
A long terrifying gaseous emanation.
Followed by someone's giggle.
I am not embarrassed by love
Or a burp or fart during lovemaking.
I hope I am not that shallow,
It goes with the territory.
In the final analysis, unless I hear
"I love you", repeated frequently,
Without the echo,
I am truly wretched.
Please make me happy,
Even if it's with a smelly white lie.

The Crocodile and the Alligator

Don't mock the crocodile or the alligator
Until after you cross the river
The brute might consider you
A delicious piece of fruit, whatever
It's just enough to make you shiver
The alligator and crocodile are certainly related.
The difference being where their teeth are located
The crocodile has gigantic teeth sticking outside his jaw
The alligator has them located on the inside of his maw
Some folks claim they love the alligator and the crocodile
It's the kind of remark that makes you want to smile
I also like the alligator and the crocodile
But only at a distance, something like a mile

Night Passage

The nights dissolve into morning
I leave your arms and thighs reluctantly
For the day's torments,
Waiting to return to our bed,
Where I find my fulfillment.
My mind's eye is always filled with
Your naked sweetness.
I am smitten and there is no help,
Beyond you,
No
I am not looking, beyond you
Honestly.
It's just an expression.
Why do you say that?
Look at me,
I am not looking.
Damn!

One Time Ending

From my perch on the railroad tie,
Swallowing creosote fumes
I can see the end of the line,
My horizon ain't that far,
Believe it friend,
It's comin at me head on,
The big crash.
A big, gray diesel,
Screamin "I don't take prisoners."
I see it lickin its chops
And sneering.
"What's you goin do road rat.
Try to get out of the way.
Hey man, don't make me laugh.
You're my meat;
I'm havin you for breakfast."
I admit it's awesome
My tongue gets kinda of dry,
My breathing accelerates;
Anticipating.
But I don't shy from the inevitable.
The word FU comes to mind
But I don't say it.
I figure, I'm kind of lucky making it this far.
I figure it best to play it, like I am grateful.
When I think back and compare, it wasn't
All that bad.
My parents were loving
My sisters were beautiful.
My children were once my life.

I had a few good friends.
Marriage, a disappointment.
I found love near the end of my time.
And no pun intended.
I still want to write the greatest poem ever.
Maybe, in the after life.

The Aphrodisiac

Once upon a time,
I was asked,
Whether or not coffee was
My aphrodisiac.
I demurred politely and explained.
I am strictly visual.
If you want aphrodisiac
Show me something naked
I do not mean a plucked
Chicken or a shaved wet cat.
Female homo sapiens will do nicely,
A warm body, ample breasts,
A comparable bottom,
Just like a fertility statuette.
Now, that is a real turn on for me.
I like the whole nine yards.
Hey, everybody is different.
When my friend was asked,
If he was turned by female legs?
He replied with quiet dignity
"Those are the first things
I gets out of my way."
My friend is somewhat gross
But a realist and
I admire that in a man.
Who knows from coffee?

Keep It Simple

Hey baby!, keep it simple
Otherwise, you're goin to grow a pimple.
Because,
Once you complex it, baby
You sure as shootin goin to wrecks it.
No maybe!
It's a basic rule
Know to every fool
And you are looking at number one
Right now.
I mean right over here.
Not over there,
Say where the hell, you looking?

It's OK for you to stare
So keep it simple, baby
And you won't see no pimple
Cause,
It ain't no fun to have a pimple
Especially, were, I've been grownin mine
Hell's fire,
I can barely reach the spot
To give one it more shot
Of Kalimine
So keep simple, Baby
and you won't have no pimple
And no need for Kalimine.

The Nazarene

On the dreadful day I died,
On a cross was crucified.
When I arose sometimes later,
I was known as my own pater.
I am also known as Christ the Savoir,
By the Greeks for my past behavior.
It was said I was resurrected
In a cave where I was detected
By a stranger sitting there,
Where I had been placed with loving care.
When my true identity was questioned
Someone in that moment mentioned
That they should put me all together
With words on paper bound in leather.
Thus, the new testament came into being
While one could hear the martyrs screaming.
In my honor and without surprise,
My apostles had me deified.
So with grim determination,
Was born a mighty Christian nation.
Thanks in main to Mark, Matthew, Luke
And John.
Whereupon, in 325 AD Peter become
My first Don.
Still, it was argued who was the true me.
David's heir or Pharisee,
A father, son and holy ghost,
With my mother playing host.

A God or Trinity of grand dimension,
With all my sects in fierce contention,
Asking if I am one or am I seven.
Alas,
Not a word was heard from heaven.
Now you know who I am,
The celebrated sacrificial lamb.

The World Ain't What It Seems

The world ain't what it seems, I grant you that
It may be nothing more than a collection of bad dreams
So hold on to your hat,
If it contains your head tuck it under your arm and
go to bed
For what I've got to say will surely knock you dead
Some say, the Universe is one big holographic illusion
Something like that
Or maybe some other kind of a strange bizarre delusion
Of your neighbor's tom cat
I kid you not,
Now, I guarantee that ain't my personal conclusion
Cause I ain't got a single clue
Of what is right or of what is true.
Now talk about a credibility gap
Hey, by now you must think me full of sap?
It's none too kind to nail you with that kind of rap
No, it and I ain't a bunch of silly crap
And
Just because you can't see it
Doesn't mean it don't exist
Take God and the angels for instance
You can buy it now or put up your own resistance
But, I understand that both ideas ain't really new
Because such notions are only understood by a special few
Like a scientist who can only try to explain it
Cause, like I said, I ain't got a clue, to this I must admit.

Valentine Advice

Honey, I know you've got something on your mind
And I can see it's a nagging irritation
But, it's nothing that I want to explore,
I don't need that kind of agitation
Frankly, I cannot handle all that stress
Not any more
Of course, I'll listen if you insist.
I had hoped you'd give me a break
Instead of forcing me into the lake
OK, then just spit it out
And we will see what your complaint is all about.
Remember,
Everyone has got some impossible disaster
That they have to meet and master
That's life's challenge to which you must not succumb
Life is nothing to forsake
When all you've got is a moment's heartache
You got to grab life's calamities by their scruffy hair
And you say, hey buster, "you wouldn't, shouldn't dare!"
And then I'd throw the damn thing clear across the room
And watch it bust into a thousand pieces with a sonic boom

How To Say I Love You

I know exactly how I'd like to say "I love you"
I'd like to write the words clear across
the nighttime sky
By pushing a bunch of stars together
And watch them sparkle with each and every letter
Carrying my love message shining up on high
And for the daytime, I'd like to say "I love you"
On a rainbow stretching from one horizon to the next
Each word written in all the brightest colors
In a kind of fancy Roman text
The words would keep repeating
"I love you!"
Not very imaginative, I grant, but true
And you would know that I wrote it,
Just for you, and only you
Yeah, that's right?
So when you look up into heavens on a clear
And sparkling night
Just think of me pushing all those stars together
In one amazing display of light
Or if by chance, you come across a rainbow
And see it written there as well
Imagine what a wild and woolly story
You will have to tell.

Different Directions

I am sorry that we have to say good-bye
I thought we had a good thing going
Heah!.. No need for us to cry
It wont repair a broken heart
No matter how hard we try
Our lives are too complex for us to sort it out
We are both going in different directions
Hell that is what life is all about
And time is our enemy,
And with all its slippery grout,
That cannot hold our love in place.
I know you crave another,
Now, now,
Its no disgrace to want another in my place.
I've had the feeling several times before
But not for you, gal, but not for you.
Our lives are too complex for us to sort it out
We both are going in different directions
That is what life is all about
And time is our enemy
And with all its slippery grout,
That cannot hold our love in place.
I know you crave another,
Now, now,
Its no disgrace to want another in my place.
I've had the feeling several times before
But not for you gal, but not for you.

The Victim

Why can't I be alone
Who says, I have to answer your telephone
Or be at your beck and call
Just because you live right down the hall
And can't do a damn thing for yourself
Not at 'all

I'm not your servant or your slave
And I do not care how much you rant and rave
I am entitled to my privacy and dignity
If you don't like it then, go climb a tree
I'm an independent person, yeah!
That's me

Well, what do you want now?
I swear, if I had tits you'd milk me like a cow
No, I didn't see your TV remote,
I bet you lose it all the time just to get my goat
Man, I'd like to squeeze your pretty throat.

What is this, you want to go to a movie
Now ain't that just simply groovy.
Well, I'm not givin up my special date
To night so you can go to the cinema.
Damn it, that's not right.
Ok, Ok, stop your screamin, cheez!, you are up tight.
What movie do you want to see?
Queen of my captivity.

The Big Epilogue

I'm into the big Epilogue, now.
Into the big good bye.
Once I was part of the Prologue.
But tempus fugit
Two of my friends have passed away recently,
I'm sure to follow.
Back to the beginning.
But, when?
I don't want to know.
There is no hurry on my part.
I am not pushing it.
When I spin into the next dimension,
Will it be a moment of great exaltation,
Or a moment of bitter regret?
Hey, Fugit!
I'm not looking forward to spending the rest of my days
In the house of the Lord.
I'm more of an action guy.
Yes!
I don't want to try to satisfy 72 virgins either.
That's too much action.
Two experienced virgins.
Would be a lovely bonus in the after world.
I am not a sexist, exactly.
They don't have to be virgins
As long as they are understanding,
Maybe, even forgiving.
I don't rate my performance A+ anymore.
I'll accept anything above a D--.
I'm not a fanatic.

Not even a believer.
The hard part is,
No, it's not that part.
It's just, I don't like change.
Even one lusty lovely lady would be exceedingly taxing,
Even dangerous for an old codger.
And I don't want to create more heirs.
I especially don't like leaving my lifetime accumulations behind,
I've considered a larger box.
I spent a lot of sweat accumulating my possessions.
I don't relish the thought of
Grieving relatives, divvying up the spoils
God knows, I tried to be fair.
My will is solid,
My lawyer says so.
But lawyers lie.
I was one myself.
I should know.
Talk about lies,
I wonder,
What shall we find there, on the other side?
A final destination or another
Beckoning?
A new prologue?
Great!
While I am not anxious to view the shinny face of the Almighty,

Forever,
A couple of centuries, more or less is OK.
No, Satan is not an acceptable alternative.
I like the temperatures balmy, not blistering.
I have tried to avoid that calamity.
I was not a goody two shoes,
A sweet slipper perhaps,
I stayed for the encore
I wanted an adventure a day,
Even if it was sexually explosive.
But I didn't lie, cheat or steal exactly.
It doesn't seem right to me then
To be abandoned in a no space.
Or in a black hole.
Not fair.
Dissolved into a bundle of spinning atoms.
Sucked into a crushing vortex.
If that is not the case,
It would be down right sinful if I can't shower
In the after life.
I like my warm showers.
Any suitable accommodation would be fine:
I envision a 5 Star Hotel.
Pool, sauna and the professional massage.
A joke! Who knows?
There is the concept of soul,
Our so called essence.
Whatever that is!
I haven't really got a clue.
Unless it means the real me.
But if we live in parallel universes,
With multiple mes and yous

Who is the real me?
There is a lot of scientific conjecture on this point,
But little in the way of hard evidence.
I like concrete evidence, but not for a pillow
Atomically, we may be lost forever in the vastness of space.
Popping in and out of reality.
Like so many subatomic particles.
Boson, meson, positron, tachyon, electron?
Not a consoling thought.
It's not the way I like to be bop.
Anyway,
There are billions of mortals who seem content with what is written
In their good books.
Hey!, I'm skeptical.
So,
Should we hope for more than cosmic indifference?
I beseech THEE on bended arthritic knees,
Higher power,
Let it be so!
I know the pain of indifference.
Or do I spend a billion years
Floating amongst a trillion galaxies
"Looking for home?"
The phrase resonates with me,
"Looking for home."
There are just too many questions,
Too many answers for a quick and easy reply.
It provokes questions.
It is enough to make my head spin.

Much less my atoms.
Candidly,
I don’t like the spinning feeling,
I get dizzy with conjectures.
Guess, I’ll take a cold shower.
A sobering thought.

The Technician

The Technician stands close by,
Protecting, a Guardian,
Always behind me.
His warm breath,
I feel but cannot see.
I have conceived of him
As a White Eagle.
Fearsome of eye and claw
In whose feathery bosom
I am secure.

I am not comfortable
With the Technician
As a man
I am disposed
To find comfort in the bosom
Of a woman,
But I cannot deny him,
His eye frightens me.
It is always in profile
Stern and merciless,
But not judgmental.
We do not exchange words.
It is I who speak.
I have often felt
His wings would protect me,
Even in a plane crash.
I have wondered too
How I survived this long,

Considering my life story.
There were so many incidents,
I should not have survived.
But luck played no part,
I am convinced.
It was the Technician.

Good Riddance

Hi Frank, what's this I hear
You're leaving town for another year
Going with the band on a big city tour
Oh my, it is a lucky you!
But what am I supposed to do
You say, we'll get married when you get back
Sounds like you're shoveling wagons of manure
Into a grubby sack
By this time, I'd hoped you'd think me more mature
Than to buy that crock of empty bull
Of which you seem to be so chockfull
So when you go, just keep on goin
Don't expect me to sit around and pretend I've been sewin
I'll be out there dude!, havin one humongous ball
In a comfy bed or in an expensive mall
And he'll be big and tall and handsome too
Not short and stumpy, nothing like the likes of you
One thing about you Frank is certain
You like to leave your women hurtin
I've been expectin this kind of noise
So I've been toyin with several other boys
Yeah, while we have been playin your guessin game
I decided I didn't need your dimwitted name
So, good riddance and keep on travelin
It might keep your ego from unravelin
So when you go just keep on goin
Don't expect me to sit around and pretend I've been sewin
I'll be out there dude havin one humongous ball
In a bed or in a mall
And he'll be big and tall and handsome too
Not short and stumpy, nothing like the likes of you.

What's The Point

What's the point in loving you?
You're a heart-break through and through
And when you say you love me to
I know you just pretend you do.
What you really mean is, "I'm about
To beat up on you."
Well, baby doll, you've been succeeding way beyond your
Expectations,
Like a voodoo lady with all her secret incantations
You've pierced my heart right to its inner core
But I can't allow that to happen anymore, not anymore
Right now you're working on my loving soul
Frankly lover girl, I can't afford the heavy toll.
The verbal punishment you inflict on me is downright
wicked
You ought to see a shrink, maybe he or she
Can teach you how to kick it.
There is no doubt about it lover girl
I've got to find me another woman soon
Or find myself howling at the ever-loving moon

I Couldn't Give It Up (Greed)

I couldn't give it up
It was much too hard to find
And when I got in my grasp
I was feeling none too kind.

I felt kind of triumphant
Like I was king of the hill
And nothing could stop me,
That's for sure,
Until I got my fill

Well, they came at me from all sides
And tried to pull me down
But I let them know
That I was the king
And I was prepared to kill.

This set them back for a time
Until they regrouped
And then tried to make their move
But I anticipated what that would be
And made them all one sorry crew

But that was many years ago,
And I still own that hill
And all the surrounding realty
Because when I dispatched my enemy
I had to kill their families.
Heah, it's what you got to do.

Its what you got to do
If you want to own the hill
And all the surrounding realty
You've got to kill your enemies
And all their families,
Large and small, they've got to fall
Heah, it's what you got to do.

God Help Me

Is that you God, calling me?
Yep it's the same old sorrowful she(he).
Like a broken cork bobbing on an endless sea
Yup, I am still on the move and
Haven't found my special grove
Nor a place to hang my gear
What, I feel like is one big salty tear
Filled with this everlasting numbing fear
Like, I don't know where I belong
And I can't see where I went wrong
Must be losing my good insight
My chest feels really up tight
A plain case of soul crushing fright
Not knowin... Where I'm a goin

Please, God help me when you can
I am a very frightened helpless (wo)man
I desperately need your intercession
Or I'll become one grand depression.
Please save me from my deadly demons
They are the really mean ones
When they just hang out there
With their ugly stare
Please, God, I need your intercession
Or I'll become one grand depression.
Please, God help when you can
I am a very frightened foolish (wo)man

Once I had a family
They were as good as they could be
Then mom she up and died.
After that, everything began to slide

No glue to hold things together
Everything just blew away just like a feather

Please, God, I need your intercession
Or I'll become one big depression.
Please save me from my deadly demons
They are the really mean ones
When they just hang out there
With their ugly stare

Please, God help me when you can!

Corruption in the World

There is madness in this world
And we watched it as it uncurled
On September Eleven Twenty-O-One
It made an entire nation ill
As it dwelled upon the gruesome kill
Of all those innocents who were trapped
In the WTC and at the Pentagon in Washington DC
So many crushed to death by tons of steel
And other poisonous debris
This was Osama bin Laden's cosmic joke
For which we sent him bombs on which to croak
Representing the heavy metal of our military
It's a bloody shame
Because in our collective brain
The memory won't remain after a generation or two
Has passed
Of this brutal villainy, and this savage butchery
We have witnessed by a group of crazed Islamic
Saudis
We are often driven to extremes
By lunatics and their schemes
In the name of racial or religious superiority
They are phonies, goodness knows
Wrapped in Satan's deadly clothes
Intent to make us slaves
As they propel us to our graves.
We must resist these mad temptations
Not fall victim to their wicked machinations
We must fight this evil force
And not waiver from this course until we put all of them
In their graves.
Amen

The Light Side and The Dark Side

There is the light side and there is the dark side on this planet we call earth
And you can fill it up with pain or you can fill it up with mirth
And I don't see where I got another choice,
If I want to sing life's sweet song with the Lord's own sweet voice.
So I'm goin to live on the light side and the bright side of old mother earth
And you can take that friend for whatever it is worth.
And like old Omar says, I goin smell the roses red,
even if it is where some buried Caesar bled.
And there are just some places where I don't intend to tread.
So I'll sing me a lovely ballad and keep the music light
And spin away my troubles through each cloudy day or night
I'm not goin to dwell on painful memories that I can't do a darn thing about
I'm not diggin up old skulls just to get me all psyched out
I goin a find me a quiet corner, a place to put my bed
And write me some lovely music that keeps buzzin in my head.
I goin sing about pretty flowers, of small children and other warm and wondrous things,
Like happy puppies and playful kittens and baby birds with precious wings.

And like old Omar says, I goin smell the roses red,
even if it is where some buried Caesar bled.
And there are just some places where I don't intend
to tread.
So I'll sing me a lovely ballad and keep the music light
And spin away my troubles through each cloudy day
or night

I am Glad I Married You

He:
Am I glad I married you!
If I hadn't, I don't know what I'd do
My folks thought I was making
A big and terrible mistake,
When I announced that it was you
Who I would finally take
As my one and only bride
You see when I was young
I was given
To acting on sudden impulse
Pushing all reason to one side
And therefore had the reputation
Of a wild and woolly flake
Oh, I have the scars to prove the point
I was often a very naughty boy
And had twisted my parents' noses completely out of joint
I tried to tell them that I had finally grown up
I was a man and no longer their unruly pup
My words while comforting were not fully understood
And did not bring them the joy
I had hoped they would
My folks did not believe I could change
So dramatically,
That is
Not until they saw the happiness
You gave to me
And then it occurred to them that maybe
I had changed quite radically.

Now, that they see how wonderful
You really are
They have apologized willingly
About misjudging both you and me
And I've gratefully accepted their apology
My folks have now become your biggest
Supporter,
Now, the boastful in-laws, of a wonderful new
Daughter.

She:
Gee, I am sorry, darling the issue has not abated
But my folks, think I made a terrible mess of
marrying a so called flake who was greatly
overrated
You see your reputation was well known in these
here parts
And the stories of your activities were like a quiver
full of moronic darts
Your reputation is not so dreadful, they claim
Except it holds their darling daughter in kind of
community disdain
So if you thought yours was a final resolution
I regret to inform you lad you have only secured
one half of a family solution.

The Spider

My, you hold yourself aloof and
I don't require further proof
Of your unmistakable rejection
I knew I did not meet your rules of
Humanoid perfection
But there was no way for me to
Escape your cunning net,
It's the one you had set;
To catch a handsome prize
Then
It must have come as one sad surprise
To find me hanging there
Drying out in the open air, so to speak
A doubtful trophy, not very sheik
It was cleverly wrought, that net and
I was easily caught.
What fool said beauty counts for naught?
He lied.
Your beauty almost destroyed my fragile pride
This web I am sure was designed to ensnare
A wealthy victim for your unholy lair
And was not for ordinary brutes like me
No, I do not intend to become unruly
It is not my style, truly
My intention is to apologize for not
seeing beyond your beauty.

Reflections on the Garden of Eden of an Afternoon

Perhaps it was not the Garden of Eden.
Yet, the flowers were beautiful and
bountiful, and they were naked.
We were not
I would have preferred it otherwise.
The setting was serene.
And you were a feast,
For the eyes and the heart

We were not alone in this garden.
Aliens had invaded our domain,
Though, we paid them scant attention,
Except for one.
They were like virtual particles,
Floating in and out of space/time,
Sometimes visible; sometimes not

A watery sundial, in a lily pond graced the garden
Measuring the passage of time,
Sun drop by sun drop.
You trembled and played sexual politics,
Seeking to dominate the scene and scenery.
In a way you did and did not?

I recall another creature in this garden
Wrapped in a gelatinous robe.
Her fat butt squashed symmetrically on
A concrete slab,
Inviting lewd and cosmic thoughts of
Copulating hominids.

In my perverse vision, I saw her rump
Painted scarlet; a baboon in heat,
Or was it the metaphoric apple?
Both inviting and repelling;
Offering a compensatory distraction, as I
Lost the end game to time.

It was a generous bottom, commodious;
It suggested a vase for all the garden's flowers,
A perfect complement!
In Brazil, it is the butt not the breasts
That inflames passion.
Alas, I am not a Brazilian, more a septuagenarian.

It was in that Garden of Eden that the snake was
indicted for indecent
Exposure;
A revisionist suggests a jealous
Succubus* as accuser.

Now cry havoc and unleash the Hounds
Of lust
So two sweet souls, entwined in each
Other's blamelessness,
Can endure the joys of life and;
Condemn themselves and humanity by
Love and lunacy, to the heavenly Fatwah**.

Shout injustice and scream the Bill of
Rights for a posterity condemned to a
Lifetime of tears, because of love.

Shout cruelty! Shout irony!
A mere tribal deity who without their
Intercourse would be childless amongst
The devout gentiles;
Here guilt is elevated to an art form.
Therefore whisper, “Mea Culpa”;
And sensuously knead your flesh
Now, all is forgiven and all is lost

I felt like a failed bowerbird.
Picking oak leaves for your straw hat,
But,
You vowed to show me a book of poetry
And you did.
I am grateful.
I enjoyed the book and you and the
Afternoon,
In the Garden of Eden where all things
Are possible,
Even the shedding of resolves.

* Succubus: A sexual tormentress that invades men's dreams.
**Fatwah, a Muslin death decree imposed upon an alleged blasphemer of the faith

My Oh, Mayo

Edgar, what's this I hear,
You put mayo on a jelly sandwich?
That's a combo, I never could quite relish
Perhaps you did it to be selfish
Figuring you would not have to share
That unsavory pair?
Even if I was shipwrecked on a desert island,
Somewhere
And there was nothing in my belly
I'm not one for the mayo with the jelly.
It seems a wee bit weird to me
But then again I've never been that hung-a-ry
I suppose you're entitled to your taste
If we was all alike it would be shameful waste
Some folks claim you are a strange one
Not me, I'm above that kind of judgment call
And your weirdness doesn't faze me, not at all
I suspect though
You don't know which one of your fingers is the
thumb
You say, "you ain't got no thumbs".
Man, even monkeys and gorillas got thumbs
Maybe that explains why your teeth and gums
Do not reject the mayo on the jelly
And just let the nauseating mix
Slip past your lips without a hitch.
I hate to tell you where I think your brains is
located
You already know?
How come?
Your mother said you are sittin' on them

Well that explains, the dumb!
I'm sorry son,
I do not think there is more than one
Active brain cell in your tiny head
Otherwise, you likely would be dead
No, I am not trying to insult you
Whatever gave you that stupid idea?
Of course, I'm insulting you,
Wake up and smell the mayo
And stop playin with your yo yo.

The Coincidence

You said you know me.
But,
I don't remember seeing you before.
You say, I know your name
And know who you are
Then why can't I recall,
Although,
Your face,
Does have a familiar cast.
Did you have it altered to hide some old
Disgrace?

Perhaps you are trying to deceive me.
Have some sinister plan in mind.
It wouldn't really surprise me.
You look the type,
A con man of sorts.
Smooth talking, a sly smile on your lips.
Some guy who is on the lam and doesn't
Give a damn.
Does that describe you and all your warts?

How did you get my name
And what brings you to my door?
If some old joker told you I was rich.
An easy touch, he lied right thru his teeth.
Rest assured my greedy looking friend,
I'm poor,
Land poor.
I own a lot of land for sure.

But it's in the wilds of Alberta Canada and
It's covered in black tar and some gritty sand.
I wouldn't even call it land.
Why, there is no place where anyone can stand!
Not fit for man or beast.

You want to buy this land, you say.
Well, I'll be damned.
Well, then come on in son.
Maybe we can cut a deal.
You do look like a lost son of mine.
Come to think of it.
He died, I do believe.
A decent boy, as I recall, who went off to seek his fortune.
Somewhere on the moon.
We haven't heard from him for many years;
His name was Hamilton.
You say that name is yours as well.
What a strange coincidence.
I wish my eyes were better.
And my wife alive.

Lyrics

Cry Beloved

Cry beloved cry, cry beloved cry
You're goin to miss this lovin guy
He ain't gonna stay by your side
He's gonna travel the whole world wide.

No point pretendin things are like they used to be
It's plain as dirt and any fool can see
Seein as I found you in my brother's arms
Now, I don't buy your fatal charms

No more, no more, no more I don't

Cry beloved cry, cry beloved cry
You're goin miss this lovin guy
He ain't goin stay by your side
He's goin travel the whole worldwide

There are lots of peaches in them trees
I aim to pick them as I please
You hurt me girl, way down deep
I can't forget that not even in my sleep.

No more, no more, nor more, I can't

Maybe I'll forgive my brother
If t'wasn't him, t'would ha'been another
The parson said it's better this way
It was sure to happen on another day

Cry beloved cry, cry beloved cry
You're goin miss this lovin guy
He ain't goin stay by your side
He's goin travel the whole world wide

I'm goin wear this scar all my days
I'm goin wear it until it doesn't faze
Then I'll write a sad, sad song
And ask the burning question,
How did it all go wrong?

Sweet as a Lollipop and Soft as Goose Down

She is sweet as a lollipop
And soft as goose down
She's princess on my school bus
And she ought to wear a crown
She's driving me crazy
Like I'm out of my mind
I can't focus on anything
No matter what's going down
The world could fall
Into a black hole in the sky
And I couldn't care less
Or even tell you why
I slip into a coma
When I get a taste of her scent
It's the wildest aroma
I am sure it's heaven sent
I'm afraid to walk down wind
When she's walking up
Because I get that weird feeling
The same, when I've sinned
It's the craziest feeling both in and outside
If I swore I didn't love her
You'd know that I'd lied
It's the craziest feeling both in and outside
If I swore I didn't love her
You'd know that I'd lied.

Why Did I Fall in Love with You Again?

Why did I fall in love with you again?
My very own *(sotto voce)*
It is just as painful now as it was then
Why did you call me on the telephone? *(sotto voce)*
Our lives are just too different to make
It all a go

Do you recall? I told you so, I told you so.
But when you called and said that
You missed me, was the word you used, "terribly"?
Then, I knew that I should flee
To the farthest ends of the galaxy
But how can I resist your sweet tones
There is something deep within
My bones.

So when I hear your lovely voice
I really have no other choice,
I am compelled to yield,
A tribute to the power that you wield
And a sorry victim of this crazy need
To taste your lips, to smell your flesh and
Perhaps to bleed?

All the while, waiting for your sad goodbye and
Praying that he will be, more that just another guy
Now baby, please, please don't protest,
I know better, better than the rest
How it's got to be,
You know, I've been there
Before.

Yes, I've been there before
That's for sure *(sotto voce)*
And I don't want that place, not anymore
It's filled with pain and yet, delicious memories of you
Remain,
Locked in my tormented brain.

(Repeat from the Beginning)

Everything Depends on the Price

Everything depends upon the price
I've got to pay,
Whether I go my darlin or whether I will stay
The answer is really up to you to say

Yes mam, I'm prepared to compromise
And meet you more than even half the way
I can't promise you that I can be the guy you want to remain
Or in the process, I won't go totally insane
But to keep you, sweet pea, I'll give it my best shot
And I'll even give it everything I've got
So let's hear it one more time what you
Expect from me
And then I'll tell you to what I can and cannot agree

Hey!
Everything depends upon the price
I've got to pay
Whether I will go or whether I will stay
And that depends upon what you
Have got to say

I really don't want to talk about religion
I never did know how to pray
But if it is important to you that I read the Holy Scripture
Believe me that will describe my solemn
Married picture

Now if you want talk about unholy spirits
And how the smell of booze makes you sick
I'll give up on the all-hard stuff, I swear, That's no trick,
But as for givin up, on wholesome beer,
Well my dear, now, that's another story
I don't think I can make down that slippery path to glory.

Hey!
Everything depends upon the price
I've got to pay,
Whether I go my darlin or whether I will stay
The answer is really up to you to say

No man could hope to love a woman more than I love you
I've got your flavor on my lips and on my tongue
And as for cigarettes, I'll give them up with few regrets,
they're just the same as shredded dung
And if I do not meet your crucial expectations
After I've committed to these obligations
Then I feel, maybe I'm the one that's been badly stung.

Hey!
Everything depends upon the price
I've got to pay,
Whether I go my darlin or whether I will stay
The answer is really up to you to say

It is not a simple thing to try to change a man,
not overnight
You are apt to give him one big heart attack
from all the fright
So why don't you try to do it then like I am ill and
you're a nurse.
Oh hell!
Ok, Ok, I also swear , not to ever curse,
Unless of course, you try to take away my ever-lovin beer.

Hey!
Everything depends upon the price
I've got to pay,
Whether I go my darlin or whether I will stay
The answer is really up to you to say

My Lips are Sealed

Hello, oh it's you?
Well, what do you want?
What?
Are you calling to accuse me of some
Imaginary plot?
Well, thanks a lot
That is rich and very generous of you
To speak of treachery
My lips were sealed on the night
We parted
And... No!
I have no clue who revealed
The secret of our sorry relationship
But I guarantee; it was not me
There would be no point for me
To expose a past and sick romance
That ended in such emptiness
On the off chance
That my ex-lover would have
A change of heart,
And ask me to return
To what, his loving heart?
You don't have a heart
Much less a soul,
For you our romance was
Just one quickie roll
On reflection,
That is all we really did.
Frankly, I am happy if only to be rid of you.
What? that's rot
I suppose... there is no denying
It was hot and heavy, while it lasted

No, I would not call it an orgy
I would not dignify it with that term

More a tasteless feast or a muddy squirm
Yes, you are in fact a filthy beast
Filthy, at the very least ,
I remember that, all too well.
And I recall vividly our last night together in that
Cheap hotel
When you got plastered, opened the window
And started to yell, that I was the most
Beautiful and sexy woman in the universe
And then you took my lipstick
Wrote AC loves RB, not my initials, on a sheet,
Hurled it out the window and while it unfurled
Shouted obscenities from the balcony
I recall the phone rang
It was the management.
They said you had to stop the cacophony
Or leave, and with no reprieve
You got sick and threw up
After that night; you didn't call
Not until tonight, that is, and
You have the gall to accuse me.

So after three weeks of depression
I got sick, threw up and had my first abortion.
Bye the Bye, congratulations on your coming
marriage.
I wish you and your intended the same
Grief you gave to me.

Chorus or Epilogue
I trusted you to do me right
But you were too blind to see the light
I trusted you and gave you all my love
It was everything I am
But in the end you really didn't give a damn
I should be grateful I suppose
That it all ended on this wretched note
Better than spending the balance of my life
Watching you chase every dirty petticoat

Time to Quit

It is so sad to say goodbye
I tried very hard not to cry,
When my heart was plainly broke,
Of course, it was not an ugly joke
We were simply swept up by this emotional tornado
Over which we had no logical control
And there didn't seem to be any other
Place to which either one of us could go
And so we went, passion bent, and
Each of us intent
On maximizing our own pleasure
Without a rational thought or controlling measure
Nor one thought of the consequences that might flow
Although I don't regret that this was so.
For I didn't know that I could spill
Such raw emotion on a sheet
Something I would like often to repeat
Yes, many times before I die
No, our loving was not an ugly lie
The guilt crept in and then we crashed.
I felt like I had been badly trashed
When it hit us like a brick.
For at that moment I felt very very sick.
I cannot believe that what we did was sinful
How can love be both so beautiful and so sinful?
But for both of us, it was so,
I know that we both felt it grow.
So please let's not deny it.

I found that lying to my Bill was pure torment
And I didn't like it for a single moment
I saw the hurt burning in his eyes
I knew the children saw through my convenient lies.
Perhaps the heat became too intense
For which we had no adequate defense.
It's true, we both have commandments to fulfill,
I just hope, I have the will.

The Spanish Galleon

I'm tired of honking the highways
Pushing this heap along
I'm tired of traveling the byways
Whistling a tuneless song

I need a different style of living
To make it seem worthwhile
A different style of giving
To make my life a smile

Guess, I'll buy me a Spanish galleon
And sail on out to sea
Must be a pair of bird wings
Just big enough for me

Then, I'll fly across the tree tops
I'll soar amongst the clouds
I laugh at those crowed highways
I'll shun those shoving crowds

Life has got to have more meaning
Than the automated shove
That pushes things together
But forgets about the love
Hey, you don't whistle on forever
It's got to end someday

Guess I'll buy me a Spanish galleon
And sail on out to sea
Must be a pair of bird wings
Just big enough for me.

Never Learned to Love

She(he) never learned to love
There was always something there
I just couldn't overcome.
I tried valiantly to scale that
Mountain peak
It must have been something
Awful of which she(he) would not speak
The ice storm that I stirred up
When I brought the subject up
Just froze me out
Yes, there was something in
Her(his) childhood that she (he) couldn't
Talk about.
She(he) never learned to love
There was always something there
I just couldn't overcome.
I tried valiantly to scale that
Mountain peak
It must have been something
Awful of which she(he) would not speak
I suggested we see a psychologist
Or marriage counselor, together
I said,
It would be like confronting a terrible storm,
I hoped both of us could weather
She(he) agreed many times but when
Push came to shove,
She(he) upped walked away from all my love
She(he) never learned to love
There was always something there
I just couldn't overcome.

I tried valiantly to scale that
Mountain peak
It must have been something
Awful of which she(he) would not speak
And when it ended.
It was like I was torn limb from limb
And my body dumped on the roadside,
And believe me, the feeling's grim.
Later, I understood she(he) remarried
Several times,
And then one more divorce.
But my love for her(him) all these years
Has never altered course
There is nothing more painful
Than a love that is not returned
Nothing more bitter than a love
That is spurned
She(he) never learned to love
There was always something there
I just couldn't overcome.
I tried valiantly to scale that
Mountain peak
It must have been something
Awful of which she(he) would not speak.

Put It on the Top

If you want to keep it movin
And you want to keep it hot
Then you got to move it from
The bottom and put it on the
Top.
It's a terrific golden rule
And a very useful tool
You've got to move it from the
Bottom and put it on the top
Chop, chop, chop, chop,
Chop, chop.
If you don't obey this law
Then they'll shove it down your craw
So move it from the bottom
And put it on the top
If you want to keep it hot
So move it from the bottom
And put it on the top
If you want to keep it hot
Get serious!
It's a basic to reality
A companion to finality,
That things will run amuck,
The world will become unstuck
If you don't move it from the bottom
And put it on the top.
If you don't move it from the bottom
And put it on the top.
I've seen it happen once or twice before
It was during the 3rd world war
When the politicians ignored it

And the generals claimed it didn't fit
They refused to take it from the bottom
And put it on the top
Do you hear?
They refused to take it from the bottom
And put it on the top
Then everything became unglued
And you and I was screwed
And you and I was screwed
So I stuffed it up with cotton
Yeah, I stuffed it up with cotton
Cause they wouldn't take it
From the bottom
And put it on the top.

Mr. X

Hey, girl, you're messin with my heart and mind
And the way you're doin it, ain't none too kind
I thought I made it clear when
We began
I had to be your one and only man
You seemed to understand the deal
That's what makes this conversation so unreal
I don't know about Mr. X
I don't know how he feels or what he expects
But I don't go in for sharing my toothbrush
Or my woman, if you are in fact my woman
It may be fun for you to play this game
For me it's just not the same
It is not the kind of relationship I care to entertain
So I am going to cash it in
And you can have all of him.
Or whatever else is your whim
Maybe you're trying to hedge your bet
That's cool, so let's see now what you can get,
No, I didn't say, I was giving you to him
Or him to you
That maneuver is strictly up to you
I thought I made it clear when
We began
I had to be your one and only man
You seemed to understand the deal
That's what makes this conversation so unreal
Now you say you didn't see it all that way

You thought I only wanted to have some fun,
And play,
No way!
Well, it's gone too far and now it's got to end.
I am throwing in my hand, so please call your other friend.
It may be fun for you to play this game
For me it's just not the same
So I am going to cash it in
And you can have all of him.
Or whatever else is your whim.

Movin On

Verse
Hell's fire, woman you're too much
For the likes of me
All you had to say is "I want to be free"
You could have whispered it or shouted
It's a message I would not have doubted
Frankly, I want the same kind of a deal for me

Chorus
So I guess it's time for movin on
I hope you'll miss me when I'm gone
I'll pack my bags and mark my tags
For sunny California
And maybe there, there's someone fair
Whose personality won't kill yah!

Verse
This relationship has hit bottom
Not one to which you could rightly cotton
It's a snake pit of conflictin tensions
Cause, underneath that mask of yours
Is a world of murderous intentions
I'm no angel that's for certain
But then again
I'm not the perfect villain

Chorus
So I guess it's time for movin on
I hope you'll miss me when I am gone
I'll pack my bags and mark my tags
For sunny California

And maybe there, there is someone fair
Whose personality won't kill yah!

Bridge
If I was as mean as you have claimed
Why I'd wrap me in an anchor chain
And drop me down a sewage drain
Or better yet, I'd defy an Amtrak train
But in that action I don't see no gain
Not for me, baby not for me
There ain't no gain

Chorus
So I guess, it's time for movin on
I hope you'll miss me when I'm gone
I'll pack my bags and mark my tags
For sunny California
And maybe there, there's someone fair
Whose personality won't kill yah.

There is no doubt about it, Angel face
You're a mighty pretty woman.
But the only time I feel safe, is when
I'm carryin a can of mace
And that don't fit my master plan
For a sweet soft life with a healthy tan

Chorus

The Gift

Verse
I was like a barren island floating in an empty sea
A parched and lonely island
on which there was nothing much to see
When on that fateful day, you landed on my shore.
I did not know until that time,
that life had promised more

Chorus
For I had never known what love was,
How sweet the touch of love
Until gifted by an Angel
from that special place, above.

Verse
By magic, the island was redone,
the bleak and desert landscape
blossomed in the sun.
Flowers bloomed most everywhere
and in that special light, I saw you there.
I could only stare, at the beauty
standing where, nothing stood before

Chorus
For I had never known what love was,
How sweet the touch of love
Until gifted by an Angel
from that special place, above.

Bridge
Birds filled our world with a love song.
I only prayed that nothing would go wrong.
I saw the sky was deepest blue and the stars
shone brightly through the night
I shouted "I love you" and vowed it so, to every
one's delight.
My heart was filled with ecstasy and we began to
dance.
We leapt and swirled as if we were in a trance.
You held me tenderly. I held you tenderly and
prayed that
Nothing would go wrong.

Chorus
For I had never known what love was,
How sweet the touch of love
Until gifted by an Angel
from that special place, above.

Verse
We sang and drank and pledged our love, with
each and every song.
These were songs of love and happiness, a love
that would not die,
until the sun grew cold and perished with the sky.
And when morning came,
I found my love where we had lain and thanked
the Angel once again.
for the nothing that went wrong.

Chorus
For I had never known what love was,
How sweet the touch of love
Until gifted by an Angel
from that special place, above.

I've Been Cut

Hello, yeah it's me
No, I ain't been away
I just shut off the phone
I got into this funk
And then I got dead drunk
It's better this way,
I'm ashamed to say
For the past two weeks
Yeah, I got cut and bucked
No, I said bucked
Yeah, like a chicken
Bucked and plucked.
Worked for that firm near
20 years and with no apologies
and no tears
A pink slip and a kick in the butt
It went bankrupt
No severance package,
No health plan, right
Two kicks in the can
The board and officers were stealin
Like mad, yeah
Inside dealin
Yep, very sad
With the help of their auditors,
Anderson was the dude
Allowed the ole boys to strip Enron nude
They cleaned out the treasury
Buried me and 100,000 others
In total misery
They took my youth

Stole all my savings
Left nothing but the shavings
My old firm sold out to Enron
About three years ago,
The new bunch put all my dough
In their stock and said it was solid
Like a rock
It was more like a bird
Went flyin through the roof
What a goof
It just bleeew away my money
Like all in one day
Feathers and dust,
All greed and lust
Man, I sure am bust
Enron went broke but
Left the directors
With millions in their poke
Now all I've got is a dirty sock
I can't sell it and I can't eat it,
It's another crock
Well how about you?
Same is true?
Then come on over
If you're sober
I got one more bottle left
We'll kill it or ourselves

It's Ok, Don't Worry/ She's My Wuman/ Am I Beat

It's Ok, no need to worry
It's Ok, no need to worry
It's Ok, no need to worry,
The door's closed
Just don't hurry

It's Ok, no need to worry,
It's Ok, no need to worry
It's Ok, no need to worry
The door's closed
Just don't hurry

(Repeat to a rhythmic beat, vary phrasing)

She's my wuman, and I'm her man,
She's my wuman, and I'm her man,
She's my wuman, and I'm her man,
I don't care whether you give a damn

(Repeat all with intensity, variation and ecstasy or the opposite)

Man, am I beat, yeah, it's the heat
Man, am I beat, yeah, it's the heat
Man, am I beat, yeah, it's the heat
Yeah man, It's also got my feet

(Repeat until you lose the beat)

Is Your Heart Free to Love?

It's time we had a heart to heart
You know that I've been struck by cupid's dart
Yet you seem to treat my feelings lightly
So let me ask you something, somewhat tritely
Is your heart free to love
To reach the moon and stars above
Or is there some joker waiting there who pulls the
String
That makes your heart and soul take wing?
Someone I must forever fear?
Is he(she) your master Puppeteer?
So when you say you are unwilling to commit
Should I assume it's just your playful wit?
Or is it his(her) voice I hear?
Should I consider this a last rebuff?
Perhaps our loving did not say enough.
You know you are always in my head
And losing you is what I dread
I do not want to feel that awful pain
So I have to ask you once again
Is your heart free to love
To reach the moon and stars above
Or have I lost you to your Puppeteer?

Cool Grasses

Cool grasses, sunlight at my heels
Walkin through soft winds
No need for metal wheels

Laughin at the morning sky
Drinking in sweet air
Haven't got a worry friend
Haven't got a care

You can keep those concrete ribbons
Those rivers of crushin steel
I'm lookin for a mountain top
Up where the silence heals

Give me a mountain meadow
A stream that passes through
I'll trade you one big city
And all the suburbs too

I'm tired of the yellin
And I can't abide the strife
I'm headin for the mountain top
And the satisfying life.

I'll marry a mountain woman
And build us a cozy home
We'll raise us a gaggle of children
And I won't have time to roam

I'll find some peace and quiet there
A secure and decent place to strive
Have honey bees and a veggie garden
And pray that I'll survive.

Ho Ho, Hey Hey

Ho ho, hey hey,
See how the big boys play
They buy their way.
They buy their way,
So you've got to pay
If you want to play like the big boys play
Or you got no say,
Go ask Mr. Lay
It's not just a bribe,
Just ask the guys inside
It's a campaign contribution
Latter comes the distribution
Consultation or speaking fees, gifts for their
private ladies
For a little legislation or presidential citation.
Who are we fooling
A generous honorarium, if you keep
The matter dumb
I can be bought,
So what if I'm caught
The word is mum.

Can't Think of Another Woman

I can't think of another woman
Who'd I'd want by my side
I can't think of another woman
Who'd I'd want for my bride
I can't think of another woman
Who'd I'd want to raise my kid
I can't think of another woman
Who'd I'd want to spend my life with
You are the only woman for me
Of this I have no doubt
The big question is
How do I bring this great event about?
You come from a wealthy family
Mine don't match that reality
I'm not looking for any kind of handout
I'm not a money grubbin scout
What I want for the remainder of my life
Is nothing more than an ever lovin' wife
And what she is gonna get from me
Why, it's just one ever lovin he.
Why, it's just one ever lovin he.

Cats and Dogs

A cat and dog may kiss
but are they the best of friends?
I don't think so
The fox and hounds may run together
but that is not how the
Story ends
Not by a long shot!
I don't think that our relationship
is getting any better
Than that of an English Tabby Cat
and an angry Irish setter

Can't you see?
You are the pussycat and I am the Irish setter
We fight like cats and dogs
in our never-ending wrestle
Like two trains about to collide
on a mountain valley's trestle
Playing chicken, we are, in a no win situation
That can only end in our mutual annihilation
It is not the way I thought
our grand romance would end
I had hoped that we could always
call one another friend
Well, no serious damage
has been done to our respective egos
What say we part like two sad sack
Mexican amigos.

Control Freak

Hey sister!
Do you think of me as some kind of simple tool?
A weakling who you can try to rule?
With a clever phrase or two
Well, sister I've got news, especially
For you,
I don't want to play your clever game
Not a minute more.
It's become tiresome and a total bore.
And though I've played it many times before
Reluctantly
I resent it now, yeah, bitterly
I don't know why I bought
Into your cunning system
Now go find yourself another willing victim
I am stunned by my own servility
To your domineering personality
You sound so open girl and without the slightest guile
Perhaps it's hidden in the disarming way you smile
And the purring of your melodic voice
In the beginning, I didn't have much choice
I was overwhelmed,
But now I do
I can see to the conniving heart and soul of you
You are a control freak
But with me, your future's bleak.
You had me doing all these funny little flips

To the sing song of your hypnotic lips
(And gyrations of your undulating hips)
Like I'm some trained dog or cat
But I didn't see the grand design in all of that.
Now it's a bore, as I've said before
Wait, allow me to show you to my back door.

Harry

There are guys who just love the girls
It doesn't matter what their shape
Or even how they stand or drape
Tall or short, fat or slim
If it's female, she's for him
My Harry is just like that, a kind of alley cat
He says that what he likes for starts, is
Female body parts
If she's got curvaceous hips
Then my Harry flips
He likes shapely legs attached to a chunky bun
He says a chunky bun is much more fun
Than any other one
Harry claims that a pretty face is secondary
To a sparkling personality
I don't know if he believes that… actually
And of course like most every other man
Harry is attached to the bosom glan
He claims he was bottle fed
Which explains his babyhood in my bed
Harry says, I'm his girl of girls, his ideal
He says I am truly beautiful
I can't describe how good that makes me feel
But loving Harry comes with a price
He insists that I must be extra nice
At least two times a day
If I want Harry, I guess that's the price
I've got to pay.
Sometimes, I wish Harry would just go away.

I'm a Simple Man

Chorus
I'm a simple man from a simple town
I have a simple smile and a simple frown
I speak simple words and their meaning's plain
I am far from perfect and I've caused some pain

Verse
One thing's certain I'm no brain trust
And to tell it straight, I'm no economust
But I know when up is up and down is down
And when we're gettin the run around

Verse
I'm not what you'd call a heavy hitter
I speak the truth and I'm no bullspitter.
You can take my words to your bank
And for that you've got my wife to thank
She's a damn fine woman who's stood by my side
When things got rough and I started to slide
She pulled me back from the edge of doom
And on that edge there ain't much room

Chorus
I'm a simple man from a simple town
I have a simple smile and a simple frown
I speak simple words and their meaning's plain
I am far from perfect and I've caused some pain

Verse
I make a decent living, nothing to boast
I'm not in debt, well, not like most
For this good fortune, I've got my wife to praise
She's had two kids and me to raise
I don't like lies much less liars
I want loyal friends when the time requires.
I watch TV and drink some beer
And I'm not ashamed of spillin a tear.

Like I said,

Chorus
I'm a simple man from a simple town
I've got a simple smile and simple frown
Hell, I'm pleased to meet yuh!

If You Want to Love Me

If you want to love me
And you say you want to love me
Then you got to do the lovin right
I'm not looking for some silly schoolboy
Who is just an empty fool-boy
I want a man who can do the lovin right
I'm no dumb chick
Who you think you can stick
With a line of bull
Like "it's only you that I adore"
My plate is full of that stuff, and
I'm not looking for a big bluff
I want to have my lovin real
Something I can really feel
Way down deep inside of me
Then I'll know you haven't lied to me
Just because you think, I'm on the pill,
That don't mean
I'm desperate for some cheap thrill,
You think you can provide.
No, I'm not desperate,
Let's just say... you tried
And I pushed you aside.
I am sure that won't save your pride
But my dignity, it will
It's necessary that I protect myself
From schoolboy foolishness
And men who play like fools
So, don't try to make it all a mess
Just memorize the rules

Or you're out of here
Do you hear?
Do you hear?
You're out of here!

(Repeat)

Loving You

Of course I love you
Can't you see, I love you
Isn't it etched within my eyes
Can't you see it there
And feel it there
It should come as no surprise

That you are the soul of me,
The essence and the whole of me,
The very meaning of my life
Everything I say, includes you
Everything I do, includes you
I want you for my own, my wife
(He wants me for his wife)
My thoughts and dreams are of you
The world before you was a lie
The moon and stars did not exist before you
There was nothing in the sky
Before you
The sun was just an angry glare
Before you.
I didn't care, before you
And without you, I can have no life,
Reprise:
Can't you see I love you
Isn't it etched within my eyes, etc.

Identity Crisis

Unless you have an identity
Of which you can be proud
Who are you anyway
Some nameless face in a
Nameless crowd.
You'll be sad to be alive
You'll be sad to be alive
If you're lucky to survive.
But finding an identity means
Striving to prove your worth
Unless you're the son or daughter
Of some king or queen
Then you get your identity by birth
Then you get your identity by birth
Who said that this was fair?
Who said that this was fair?
If you're a member of this elite
You'll find the paparazzi fawning at your feet
Unless you're spawning on some unmarried sheet
Then watch the TV's talking turds
Paint you with some ugly words
You'll be sad to be alive
You'll be sad to be alive
If you're lucky to survive
Some kids are sired by millionaires
And live a life without financial cares

A few are born with special talents
Who sail on to fame and fortune
Or on the names of their famous parents
But there is a cost to all of this
Something one could dread
It means the loss of privacy
In and out of bed
But, it offers lots and lots of compensation.
What us poor folk call bread
Who said that this was fair?
Who said that this was fair?

Reprise: You'll be sad to be alive, etc

A few of us become successful businessmen
(Not too many women)
Whom they call tycoon
But that is a very heady place
Where there isn't that much room
It's very tough to keep the pace
So few of us succeed
To make enough to stay alive
Not to mention, what you really need.
You'll be sad to be alive (repeat)
If you're lucky to survive. (repeat)
Who said that this was fair? (repeat)
I'm not talking about the USA,
Where there is opportunity galore
With a chance to chew some juicy chuck
If you're expert with a ball or puck
I am not slamming Western Europe

Or even that big third world
Where most folks live and die
Without the slightest hope
Of reaching the ripe old age
Of forty firggin-five
You'll be sad to be alive
You'll be sad to be alive
If you're lucky to survive
If you're lucky to survive.
Who said that this was fair? (repeat)

I Never Should Have Married That Man

Mama said that I should never go to bed with
every Tom Dick or Harry
I didn't listen to what Mama said
Now look at what I've got to carry
So sad, too bad, do-dad
Mama said I should not have taken up with Dick
or was it Harry
Mama said that he was bad for me and not
disposed to marry
Mama said if I married Harry I would suffer
Mama's right
Things couldn't have gotten much rougher
How did Mama know?
She must have called that Psychic
On the late night TV show.
Mama said that he was too good looking
And had bedroom eyes.
Mama said
So it should come as no surprise when He
disappeared.
So sad, too bad, do dad
Mama said while I was no dummy
I didn't need a swollen tummy
It wasn't very practical
Mama was right once more
She said I should choose a breadwinner before
I chose a lover
If I wanted to eat a regular kind of supper
And it was OK with her
If they was two different guys
That's because my Mama is very wise

Endlessly

If the ocean can pound the shore
And never split the sand
If the moon and stars can fill the sky
And never touch the land
If the earth can tilt and spin on endlessly

Then why won't you love me?
It's unfair, it's unfair, it's unfair

If the tides can wax and wane
And never seem to tire
If the sun can burn forever
And never lose its fire
If night can change to day

Then why won't you love me
It's unfair, it's unfair, its unfair.

It seems like such a simple thing to do
Compared to nature's wonder
To make her love me
Not call for rain and thunder.

I'll give it one more whirl or two
And if it doesn't work this time

I'll try what Adam did before me
And try a rib of mine

Refrain

No use to fret and cry
For a love that won't take hold
I'll go and find another before
I'm too damned old.

A Kind of Distance

I could never figure out what you wanted.
I could never figure out what you had to hear.
I always lost my way with you,
Trying to be honest and sincere.
It was not that I believed I would ever lose you
You were never really mine to own
You were always a kind of mystery to me
I knew you were more or less on loan
You always kept a distance from me
I could see it in your face
When we were making love
In that most intimate embrace.
And now you say you are leaving
I still don't know the reason why.
I don't want to see the only thing
I've ever wanted shrivel up and die.
So, don't go away and leave me
What will I ever do?
For I don't believe it's possible
To find another love, like you.
For I don't believe it's possible
To find another love, like you.
(Repeat the Lyrics)

Wait For Me

No one owns Mr. Time
He goes his lonely way, and
He won't hear your tormented cry
If you should ask for one more day
No!
Not even for one more minute.

So why didn't you wait for me
Like you said you would.
I told you that I would return,
No matter what
And we would wed
And then you said
I'll wait forever, if I must.
It won't be forever,
I promised
Maybe a year or two,
No more, I trust
And you said,
I'll wait an eternity, my love.
Your words echoed in my head
So why didn't you wait for me
It was only for another month or two,
No more.
I didn't say another year
Who frightened you and filled your heart
With mindless fear
That I would not return.
Was it your mom or dad,
I hope not, it would be much too sad

For me to grieve
That I lost you to a foolish peeve
I wrote you everyday and
Spoke my soul and
Sped E-mails on their way
And you replied and we renewed
Our pledge of love each and every day.

So why didn't you wait for me
Now you've made a wreck of it
He married you or not.
No one knows whether
You and he tied the knot.
Or was it just a mindless fling?
I understand that he filled your body

With a living thing
I hope for your sake he did it with a ring.
God knows, how I wanted you
So why didn't you wait for me.
It means I have to start anew
I do not want to, God knows,
I do not want to
But what else is there to do.

Reprise

With You Everything Is Personal

He
Wow, time out, we've begun to shout,
Our simple arguments have become battlegrounds
Where everything is personal and filled with ugly sounds
Reason is stretched into gross distortions
Way beyond all reasonable proportions
We seem to heatedly debate the simplest of questions
It's enough to cause a body all kinds of painful indigestions
You argue like some despotic ruler
Whose attitude toward lesser mortals couldn't be much crueler
You swell up in one gigantic huff and order all our heads cut off
I cannot abide such flagrant miss-behavior
It's the kind relationship no gentleman would favor
I prefer a friendly disagreement followed by a kiss
Or I fear, my love, you will always be a Miss

Chorus
You will always be a Miss,
You will always be a Miss
Unless you remember this,
Unless you remember this
That an argument is never lost or won
If all the parties are having fun,
If all the parties are having fun
The argument is never lost or won
And if you can keep responses light you will avoid a bitter fight,
You will avoid a bitter fight, if you can keep the responses light.

She
Why you supercilious son of a witch,
Who do think you are,
Some gentleman, Har! Har! Har!
You don't know what the word means,
You are so full of beans
You are telling me if I do not agree with thee,
I'll end up as a Miss,
Well buster, get this.
If I end up as a Miss so will you, if you get my drift
I'll make short shrift of the family jewels or whatever you call those
Smallish tools hidden in your jeans.
You won't have to pretend you're a gentleman unique
When I get done with you, you will be a unique eunuch,
I may still be Miss
But I won't be missing any fun and as for a friendly kiss
You know where and what you can kiss
Hey, I'd be thrilled to guide you there.
Well I'll be galled, you are going bald.

A Duet Song in a Sing-Song

Sung by Melanie and Marty like the sing song in The Umbrellas of Cherbourg

Mel Honey, don't you think Michael is very sweet?

Mar What? I wasn't tuned in. Please repeat.

Mel I said, don't you think Mickey is very sweet?

Mar What is that supposed to mean?

Mel That is supposed to mean, don't you think Michael is very nice?

Mar Yeah, very sweet and very nice, but he's not my kind of treat. Me, he don't entice. Wait a minute, are you saying that you think, maybe I am gay?

Mel Well, gay or nay, it's wonderful to be admired by a man, any man even half a man whether he's gay or straight. Don't you agree? And if Mickey looked at me the way he looks at you, I'd be hooked. It's not too late to your change luck. Gay or straight you are still a handsome buck.

Mar That is hitting way below the belt.

Mel Oh, I'm sorry, I didn't think there was anything below your belt, except hot air or I wouldn't have tried to hit you there.

Mar I resent your sarcasm and your spiteful innuendo.

Mel Well, I don't know about innuendo but I do know you haven't been very attentive, of late. And the way Mickey looks at you in such a hungry state, I swear, I thought

maybe you'd prefer to share, your nights
if not your days with him or he or do you
have a lady or gentleman parolee for whom
you care who would love to search your
underwear?

Mar That is cruel, you know I love you bitch

Me Then why don't you try and scratch my
itch?

Mar What do you mean, why don't I show it?

Mel You haven't made love to me these past
three months.

Mar Three months, it cannot be. Well, if so and
I'll not admit it I have had other things on
my mind and sex was not a priority.

Mel That maybe be true among a gentlemanly
minority and specially so, if you are getting
it elsewhere.

Mar That is damned unfair.

Mel Is it? And since when is sex not a priority.
Why it is the foundation of a happy
marriage and a baby carriage. It is the stuff
that keeps the grass growing, world turning
and the balls glowing.

Mar Not in my world.

Mel Then you should see a psychiatrist maybe
he or she can untwist that head of yours
and see what going on inside.

Mar Ah! another jibe, or to quote Shakespeare
"she jests at scars who never felt a wound"

Mel How about "he jests at scars because he
hasn't felt my womb?" Not for months
Anyway.

Mar I do not think that's very funny?

Mel It isn't funny, and wasn't intended to be and if you haven't got time for me, perhaps you'd prefer little of Mickey and his big or little dicky.

Mar That hurt, that really hurt!

Mel Well, I want my marriage to work, and if we can't talk about it then the problem will never will be resolved.

Mar I hate my job and if I can't pull out of it, I'll curl up and dissolve.

Mel Marty dear, I am willing to help you, but don't die on me, not now. I'll do everything I can, just tell me how? Better yet, let's write a skit. I have this great idea, let's just do it.

Why Can't I Write the Perfect Song?

So, why can't I write the perfect song?
Why is it that all my words and sounds go wrong?
When I lift my voice to sing
To tell the world about this thing
I have for you.
The words and music don't ring true
And this makes me very sorrowful and very blue
It's like I am completely superficial
And what I have to say sounds so completely artificial
So, why can't I write the perfect song?
Why is it that all my words and sounds go wrong?
Other writers seem to say, "I love you",
And do it very well!
When I try to say it, its like I drowned them all
In some deep artesian well
The words and music come out dripping wet
Very soggy, soaked in sincere regret
It's like I've had too much to drink,
Hey! what else am I to think?
Maybe one day, it will happen by pure accident
I'll write song and it will say, "I love you"
And you will know the words and music
Are everything that I have meant
Because they sound like they are absolutely true
And were crafted especially for you
So, why can't I write the perfect song?
Why is it that all my words go wrong?

The Good Life or Miss Jezebel

I tried to live the good life, the good life, the good life
The way the good book says I should.
I tried to live the good life, the good life, the good life
The way the good book says I should.
Then I met Miss Jezebel
And took damnation trail
Directly into hell
Then I met Miss Jezebel
And took damnation trail
Directly into hell
Gave up my family and friends I did,
Ripped off my boss
Stole money from my wife
And even from my kid,
I'm ashamed to say
I lusted for her night and day,
Miss Jezebel
The lovin was oh so very sweet; we did it every way
On this musty, dusty road to hell
I tried to live the good life, the good life, the good life
The way the good book says I should.
Then I met Miss Jezebel
And took damnation trail
Directly into hell
I swear, I was possessed by some evil spirit
Body and soul
Like I was on some fiendish, hellish kind of roll
And in a crazy way, I must admit
I enjoyed it, I enjoyed it every bit
Then, one day, it just ended
She just upped and left

Damn right, I was offended
She left me deep in debt,
My credit, it was ruined,
My life, it was a wreck and
I'm not ashamed to say, I wept and wept
Sorry for myself, I was
Until, I heard from the local fuzz
She took her boss for 100 thou
She was doin us both, the devil's sow
I tried to live the good life, the good life, the good life
The way the good book says I should
But then I met Miss Jezebel
And took damnation trail
Directly into hell
Did I learn my lesson?
I hope, I'll never know
Because, if she walked in that door.
No tellin which way I'd go.

Come Back To Me

Come back to me, you didn't have to go away.
Come back to me, I wanted you so desperately to stay
I am so sorry for the misunderstanding
I didn't mean to sound so damn demanding,
If that is the only reason that you left.
Come back to me, without you life is total desolation.
Come back to me, I cannot live in such deadly
isolation.
I will despair and one will care,
What happens to me or you.
Just to say the words, "I love you"
Cannot speak of all the raw emotions
I draw from you.
If you don't come back,
I know that I will burn in a hell of my own creation
Who but a fool like me would create his own
damnation
And that is not what I wish to do
To live a hellish empty life without the nearness of you
So please, come back; forgive this empty soul
Your forgiveness is his only goal.

Can I come home? I am sorry that I left.
And left you all alone
Can I come home? without you I am bereft.
Can I come home? you must have accidentally
disconnected
The telephone.
I cannot reach you, to beseech you please let me come
home.
I do not recall what our argument was all about.

All I can remember was the ugly shouting,
Yet never doubting, my eternal love for you.
Please beloved, let us both forgive, for I cannot live
A moment more without you.

You Led Me On

You led me on, you led me on, you (S)DOB
And I followed blindly, like an ordinary fool
Who didn't realize, he/she was being used
Like some common variety garden tool
God, I hate to be violated in such a callous fashion
By someone who knows how to fake (her/his) passion
A victim's game is what you played on me,
So you could get the attention of Mr./Miss ABC
An obvious Orangutan and low IQ'd
Now, you made me look some pathetic jackass,
A pitiful dupe.... who's just been screwed.
I was only saying to my family and friends
How this was it, I was out of the singles' loop
You and I were the perfect fit!
Instead, I end up face down in a pile of.... dirt
You can figure how much that can hurt
When you learn you have been rejected
For one grade a creep,
Your choice makes me feel so damn low and so damn cheap
So let me bring you up smart and short
And offer you one small bit of cold comfort
It ain't over till it's over lover dear,
And what goes around comes around
And that gives me a tiny bit of face saving cheer!
Chorus

If I Had Known

I did not know what I had missed for all those years
Until that moment when we first kissed,
I shed my tears
For were it so, so early on
I might have changed my life, forever
To what ends would I have gone
And how different things would have been
Had we lived a life of sin
A life of love with you, and only you to treasure
For you and me, now at least there is no pain, and
no more grief,
Not more to gain, then simple love and pleasure
If only just to be together,
But that was not how our lives were laid,
Nor how the moments of our lives were played,
Until that very moment,
When, you became my fate.
It was worth the wait.
Yes, it was worth the wait.

She's a Little Mama

She's my little mama, perky and bright
Tho, I swear,
She wears her jeans a might too tight
But
I love to watch her when she spins on by
Catching every guy's glances but no one's eye

Well, I'm proud to say she is sort of mine
At least I think so, most of the time.

She got a shapely bottom and an ample bust
And although she talks kind of common,
She's a real brain trust
She tries to hide her smarts behind a ready wit.
Cause she likes that scene where all the pieces fit.
She has a gorgeous smile and two sweet lips
When she kisses, man, it makes my heart do flips

Well, I'm proud to say she is sort of mine
At least I think so, most of the time.

Now when she walks across a room the lights go ape
The bulbs seem to know her and her outstanding shape
And they seem to bounce and flash all over the place
And it gives my club a special kind of grace

Well, I'm proud to say she is sort of mine
At least I think so, most of the time.

Now no sane person would dispute my claim
I stand six foot four and fill a large door frame

I got ham hock hands they almost touch the floor.
It's the kind of fists that can make men sore.

Well, I'm proud to say she sort of mine
At least I think so, most of the time.

I'm In Love With Santa Claus

As you grow up, as you grow up
There are many things
You leave behind
And soon forget

All sorts of silly toys
That once belonged
To tender little girls and boys
But it is also clear
That there are
Memories dear
You can't forget
When you grow, when you grow up

I'm in love with Santa Claus
I hope he's in love with me
One Christmas Eve I dreamed I saw him
He was dressed in red and white
And he was shinning like a star
In a wondrous soft light
The light was like a halo
Surrounding his white hair
And the living room seemed to glow
So I tried hard not to stare
Santa had a kind and gentle face
And yet he looked like someone
From every other race
I offered him hot cocoa
But, he shook his bearded head
And in a mellow voice he said

“No, I cannot stay, I’ve got to go
There are little children everywhere
Waiting for the gifts I bear
No, I cannot stay
I simply must be on my way.”
And as he left, I heard him shout
“I love you one and all.”
And for the moment I was struck
By a just single thought
Isn’t that what Christmas
Is really all about?
Then I saw him disappear
Into the Christmas night
I shouted back
I hoped that he would hear
“I love you Santa Claus
And losing you is what I fear.”

How Could You? (Geezer Song)

How could you marry that old man?
His skin reminds me of a can of uncooked spam
They say his mother was some dorky chimpanzee
And his father couldn't recite the alphabet from A to P
Ain't you got no family pride?
To let that old chimp lie down by your side
Well, just because he can pay a fancy upscale rent
On your New York penthouse apart-a-ment
Is no reason to sell yourself so cheap.
To some rich old dotty Wall Street creep
Huh?
He also bought you a 3-carat diamond ring,
Before he wed you?
And he called it a mere bauble and a nothing thing
Before he bed you?
You say
You spent your honeymoon sailing on his private
Yacht!
And
He gave you a beige Mink coat and a Mercedes Benz
To match!
Cruising the Florida coast and Puerto Rico were you
With his old buddies and their young bimbo squeezers,
With you?
Maybe, I've misjudged the dear old geezer
Ask your darling spouse, if he has any more
senior friends
Who are in the market for real geezer pleaser.

LaVergne, TN USA
22 June 2010

187064LV00004B/39/P

9 780962 931130